Fashion Doll Makeovers III

by Jim Faraone

Learn from the Artists

Faraone Originals

Published by

Hobby House Press, Inc. Grantsville, MD 21536

DEDICATION

To my father and mother, Albert and Florence Faraone, for their patience and understanding.

ACKNOWLEDGEMENTS

My deep felt thanks to all the featured artists/designers for sharing their time and talents with us; my father and mother, Albert and Florence Faraone, for their support; Charles Faraone for his computer expertise; Kerry Anne Faraone for photographing the "How To" section; David W. Simpson for his belief in me when I was first starting out; Barbara and Dan Miller of *Miller's Fashion Doll* magazine and Beth Owens for their support; Karen F. Caviale and Marlene Mura of *Barbie® Bazaar* for their support of the artists; Helga Hubmann for her help with the foreign artists; Denver J. Yorton CPhT, Dave Styles, Right Rev. Jason R. Mulhall, D.D, D. Min, Matt Gardner, Tony Fay, Tom Agner, Linda Love and Tom Potts for saving my sanity in busy times.

Photo by Albert Faraone, Sr.

ABOUT THE AUTHOR

Jim Faraone is an avid doll collector with a collection of more than 3,500 dolls of all kinds. He also collects paper dolls, paper toys, 40s and 50s plastic dollhouse furniture, the 60s Ideal® Petite Princess dollhouse furniture, children's tin cookware and accessories, celebrity autographed photos and more!

A respected artist, Jim has had his artwork featured twice in the UFDC (United Federation of Doll Clubs) publication *Doll News*. His award winning artwork has also been featured as souvenirs at many conventions and has been on display at the Metropolitan Museum of Art in New York City.

Jim has also created, along with Barb Rausch, the first *Fashion Doll Makeovers Paper Doll Book*, which was the top souvenir of the 1999 National Paper Doll Convention. This paper doll book features two dolls and 17 outfits designed by some of the artists from his books.

His articles on the *BARBIE®* doll and paper dolls have appeared numerous times in several magazines. He has also covered many of the conventions in magazines and on the Internet.

Jim is internationally known in the collecting field and is actively involved with many of the conventions. He organizes and runs many of the Artist's Galleries that feature the new work of professional and non-professional artists. Jim is an avid believer in supporting artists and giving them the recognition that they deserve. He has presented several workshops on topics such as painting techniques, paper doll artwork, getting published, and the recreation of the fashion doll.

Jim has appeared in several magazines and newspapers around the world, including the front cover of *USA Today*.

His recreated fashion dolls have also appeared on several television news segments as well as in magazines and newspapers. His one-of-a-kind AIDS Awareness *BARBIE®* doll auction donation, dedicated to three collectors at the 1998 *BARBIE®* doll convention in Atlanta, Georgia, brought in over $3,500 for the charity. He likes variety, so he creates everything from Haute Couture ensembles, caricature dolls and vintage suits to hand beaded and sequined evening gowns. His intricate beadwork has astounded many collectors who own one of his detailed creations. All of his full-skirted creations have tiny lace-trimmed panties, a garter belt with rhinestone "clasp" and stockings beneath the flowing skirts. He enjoys adding the small detail work on his creations. For Jim Faraone, the joy, comfort, and friendships he has made over the years are always treasured. He truly enjoys hearing from collectors and artists around the world. Feel free to contact him with any comments or feedback on his books.

Jim Faraone
19109 Silcott Springs Rd., Purcellville, VA 20132
(540) 338-3621 • Email: jimfaraone@erols.com • Web site: http://www.erols.com/jimfaraone/

Additional copies available at $19.95 plus postage from
Hobby House Press, Inc.
www.hobbyhouse.com
1 Corporate Drive
Grantsville, MD 21536
1-800-554-1447
E-mail: hobbyhouse@gcnet.net

ISBN: 0-87588-554-3

Table Of Contents

Introduction

I am proud and honored to be back with my third book featuring more talented individuals from around the world and taking you a step further in creating your own fashion doll wonders.

As you know, I am constantly in search of artists/designers to be featured in my books. Many have written or E-mailed with questions and I have been more than happy to respond personally to each one. Here are the two most frequent questions that I receive:

Q. How can I be a featured artist in one of your books?

A. To be considered for one of my books, all you have to do is send me at least three (3) photos of your creations for my files. I keep a file on each artist who sends me photographs. The day the publisher approves a book I open up all the files and begin to select who will be invited to be included in the new book. It's probably the toughest decision in creating a book! Those who do not make it into a book are then held to be considered for future books. (The decision on who to include is based on both the number of artists and the attempt to vary the styles as much as possible.) Once I have a file on an artist, I keep it always, so I hope that artists who have already sent material will update their photos and address changes every few months. Why not send me your photos now and get a place in my files!

Q. If I send you photos, will you critique my work?

A. I am always willing to help out wherever I can, but do not critique work since it may crimp the artist's style. I believe in originality and that all designers/artists should create from their hearts.

I will give tips, though, on what to do to make creations stand out:

First, the quality of your workmanship should be the best you can do. Practice makes perfect! No one has become a sensation overnight. It is important to work at it, and work hard. If you're going to do a rush job just to make a lot of dolls, or make dolls to trade with others so you can get better dolls in your collection, it will reflect on you. Take your time with each creation, for what counts is quality and not quantity. When working on outfits, iron along the way, for it will eliminate the bulges and bumps in your outfits. Use fabrics that are in proportion to the doll. Don't take shortcuts because they will only show up in the end.

Accessorizing is important to me! I have seen some lovely outfits, but it ends there. Although the outfit may be pretty, you should strive for knockout! Add the gloves, bags, hats, stoles, jewelry, accessories, or whatever necessary, and finish those outfits completely. Even if you're into a Gothic or punk look, get down to the details and study the jewelry, hair, piercings or any other minute detail that will enhance your creation. You will definitely see a world of difference when you totally finish a doll.

For example, I have created a doll to show what she looks

like without her accessories and the amazing transformation that takes place after she gets the finishing touches.

Once again, note that the artists featured are not affiliated with the companies that produce and manufacture the dolls on which their fashions are displayed. Though enhanced, these dolls are merely used as mannequins.

Don't be reluctant to contact me or the artists featured in this book. It is through positive communication and constructive criticism that we will grow in the millennium.

Jim Faraone
19109 Silcott Springs Rd.
Purcellville, VA 20132
(540) 338-3621
E-mail: jimfaraone@erols.com
Web Site: http://www.erols.com/jimfaraone/

Read on...

Dolls are magical caricatures of people. With their beauty, grace, and expressive faces, dolls remind us of a never-never land of nostalgic childhood memories, a place many of us had to leave behind as we grew up. To many collectors, dolls represent a return to the world of innocence.

This book showcases artists' interpretations of beauty and love for dolls. As you look at the hundreds of different examples and consider how you wish to design your own doll - face, hair, costume, accessories - the author and publisher would like you to do the following:

• CAUTION - Any change to the originality of a doll can influence its resale value to a collector on the secondary market. We therefore suggest that you use a much loved and much played with doll in your artistic endeavor. Using these "hurt" dolls is rescuing and preserving them for future generations. If you cannot find much loved or played with dolls, then use newly made dolls.

• Always sign and date your work. This makes your design an original and insures that all your hard work and dedication will be recognized.

• Represent the sale of your work as coming from you the artist - never represent yourself as "Jim's *BARBIE*® doll and outfits", "Ginger's *Gene*® dolls", etc. Although you have created your own design for a fashion doll, that fashion doll was originally created by, and the rights to the doll belong to, someone else. Include a disclaimer such as the following in your advertising and show displays: (Doll name) is a trademark of (Company name). This (These) doll(s) is (are) not sponsored by or affiliated with (Company name).

• Most importantly, enjoy yourself and let your creative juices flow!

Sandi Alex

Creations by Sandi Alex
Photos by Stephanie Anderson and
Richard Blomberg

"So, where does a small-town, stay-at-home mother of three find creative fulfillment? On the Internet, of course!

I have always been a doll lover. From my earliest memories of the *Chatty Cathy*® doll to my first *Bubble Cut BARBIE*® doll, my dolls have always been a big part of my life. Although my *BARBIE*® dolls were my play dolls, the sanctified space behind the glass in the cabinet belonged solely to Madame Alexander. My Alexander dolls were, by far, what made up my definition of a quality doll; elaborate costuming, no detail overlooked and quality material. I simply adored them. I was never allowed to play with them, but to look fondly at them was enough for me...then!

I was forced to sell my Alexander collection in the early 80s in order to make the down payment on our first home. Although it was a heartrending decision, I knew I was doing the right thing. For the next 15 years, I couldn't even look at a doll; the memories were just too painful for me. One day, a friend asked me to accompany her to a doll show, and the minute I walked in the door, I knew I was hooked all over again. I collected in a mad frenzy, making up for 15 years of lost time. I was even able to locate some of the dolls from my old collection and redeem my favorite doll from my childhood.

About this time, I joined the Internet and found some wonderful fellow collectors. Some of these rogue friends of mine decided to shed their girls of their factory clothes, tags and boxes and actually have fun with their dolls! Although I have been sewing for 25 years, I began to be exposed to some of the wonderful on-line doll seamstresses. Their creative work just spurred me on to try some things I'd never tried before. I started with some vintage *Cissy*® doll patterns, and eventually began developing my own patterns. The *Cissy*® doll is such a blast to sew for; she can pull off just about any style and she's such fun to pose. Another great model in the Alexander line is the *Coco*® doll. She's a wonderful size (16in), and once you get her out of the pink she usually comes in, her natural good looks just take off. My favorite girl and specialty, however, is the *Cissette*® doll. This 10-inch petite beauty has all the features that I love: classic good looks, quality construction and great dimensions. The vintage *Cissette*® dolls are easy to pose, and it's a breeze to store and display dolls of this size. I definitely would not recommend starting out sewing for the *Cissette*® doll, however. Begin with the bigger girls, and work yourself down in size as you hone your skills.

In regard to dressing dolls, however, let me caution you not to take just any mint-in-the-box MA doll, rip its clothes and tags off and devalue it. There are plenty of less than mint dolls on the secondary market that are just waiting for a makeover. Another

SANDI ALEX
1005 NE 6th Ave.
Camas, WA 98607
E-mail: GRRRALEX@aol.com

practice that is becoming popular is "splitting" a doll, that is, to buy a doll, keep her for redressing and sell her outfit. Doll splitting is a cost-effective way to purchase one of the modern *Cissy*® dolls and is common practice among my on-line friends.

Although I am an Alexander purist, I enjoy checking out all the wonderful things that are being done with the *Gene*® doll and the *BARBIE*® doll. I'm always speculating on how I can transfer some of their creative ideas to my Alexanders. I'm especially intrigued by some of the *Gene*® doll's vintage fashions. We Alexander collectors are just now realizing how much fun our dolls can be to play with.

I don't think that you can spend as much time sewing as I do without a supportive family. My husband and sons are extremely understanding, even when they step on the occasional pin or needle. We've all learned to live with bits and pieces of material in every room of the house. They pretend not to notice as I patiently pick threads off my sweater during church. My dear boys don't really 'get' their mom's strange doll hobby, but they have allowed me the time and space to pursue it to the best of my ability.

My cardinal rule of sewing has always been to never turn down a challenge. I've taken on some projects that no one else would touch, and have thoroughly enjoyed the experience. Every new ensemble I make teaches me something new. I hope to be learning and sewing for a very long time."

Dennis Beltran

Creations by Dennis Beltran

"I have been collecting and restoring dolls for over three years, but have been making cloth dolls since I was around ten years old. The hobby was a joint effort with my best friend and together we made dozens and dozens of different dolls, experimenting with many ideas. The dolls had cloth bodies and Styrofoam heads coated with plaster to get rid of the porous look of the Styrofoam. This dollmaking hobby included animating them to music in short film/videos.

We used *BARBIE*® doll clothes and went to extremes to get *BARBIE*® dolls from neighbors and relatives. The dolls became donors and were scalped, then we would transplant the scalp onto the dolls we made. Primitive rerooting, I guess. After a while we began to really study the *BARBIE*® doll and we began a small collection of the 80s *BARBIE*® dolls and *Jem*® dolls rescued from thrift stores. My friend stopped collecting but I kept going.

It seemed only natural to want to give them all separate looks to differentiate each doll's character. Hair style seemed to be the most obvious and easy way to change a character's look...makeup was soon to follow. Although I have always been into customizing dolls, I never really concentrated on that aspect of collecting, or even realized where it could take me until after I started collecting the vintage *BARBIE*® dolls. I experimented with restoring them as close to original as I could, using the faded lines and hair parts. When I could afford books on vintage and actually saw photos of the dolls, I realized my intuition with dolls was pretty good.

My first *BARBIE*® dolls were a bunch of TNT's that I traded for several of the then new and rarer brunette 35th Anniversary reproduction ponytail *BARBIE*® doll. It was the reproduction doll that opened my eyes to the vintage *BARBIE*® doll. Before then, I had never known that the *BARBIE*® doll ever had any other face than the toothy grin she haunted me with all through my childhood.

Among my first dolls was a brunette #5 ponytail in grotesque condition which I repainted with #1 eyes and rerooted with waist-length red hair in the vintage style ponytail. I gave the doll away to one of my first restoration customers and it was sold for around $75.

I think doll customizing is a popular hobby because it allows for people to obtain dolls they want without having to look for them and spend lots of money on them. When I see a doll, I can see what it will look like when it is done and so the pressure is on to make the doll meet the standards in my head. Dolls can usually take me as much as months to finish or sometimes as little as 10 minutes depending on how stubborn the doll is. This hobby is a good way to have what you want and also be able to say you had a part in making it. Seeing how different a face-mold can look using paint styles is extremely fascinating."

Marilyn

DENNIS BELTRAN
1565 West Ave. Apt. #207
Miami Beach, FL 33139
E-mail: YManno@aol.com

Laurie Berger

Creations by Laurie Berger

"Hi! My name is Laurie Berger, I'm 21 and I'm French. I live in Nantes, a big town in the west of France. When I was young, I had a lot of *BARBIE*® dolls like all little girls did! But over the years, my passion increased! I began to collect and create for the *BARBIE*® dolls. As I always have new ideas and love to draw, I note my ideas down and create them when I find the time. Everything inspires me: movies, art in general, history, nature, stars (Kate Winslet, Jennifer Aniston, Spice Girls...). My sister asked me to create some dolls that she had sketched and now, all the cupboards are full and there's no place for anything else!

In France, there aren't many choices in dolls, so I have to color their hair with a special ink (Standard Speedry Magic Color), repaint their eyes and lips and even remold their arms. My latest ideas are to make Lara Croft, Friends actors and some heroes of Manga (Japanese comic strip)."

Tout Feu Tout Flamme.

LAURIE BERGER
7 rue du Général Buat
44000 NANTES
France

Crystaline Fairy

Copacabana *BARBIE®* doll

Jeanine L. Black/ Anthony C. Klosky

Creations by
Jeanine Black/Anthony Klosky

"I was born in Chicago, Illinois and still live in the north suburbs. I have three children, ages 23, 18 and 4.

My love for the *BARBIE®* doll started as a young child when I spent many hours looking over her fashion booklets. I would sketch out her fashions, making my own interesting changes, but only on paper because I was too young to sew them. I would dream up the most unusual designs. That dream wouldn't be realized until I was much older and learned how to sew. I started making my own clothes in junior high school. After I was married and had kids, I made clothes for them as well.

My daughter Kristen is an ice skater, and for many years I made elaborate skating costumes for her, and other moms wanted to enlist my services. It gave me great pleasure to see the skaters wearing my designs and to be acknowledged as the best costume designer by the parents. My skating costumes were seen at skating competitions all over the country. My daughter is now

coaching and no longer competing, so my attention and sewing ability shifted over to the *BARBIE®* doll.

After so many years of sewing for a normal-size person, suddenly making clothes to fit a 3-inch waist was a little difficult at first. After many mistakes and some frustration, I finally made the transition. Designing and constructing the fashions for the *BARBIE®* doll is exciting and challenging. I can live out my own fantasies through the *BARBIE®* doll, but wouldn't dare. The *BARBIE®* doll is the ultimate fashion model, and wouldn't we all love to look like the *BARBIE®* doll?

Last year I started working for our local Wal-Mart store, where else but in the fabric and craft department? I had been working on a bride doll and decided to donate her for one of the many charitable fundraisers that Wal-Mart does. The doll was raffled for our local fire department to purchase a special helmet. The doll realized about $2,500 and I was thrilled beyond belief and felt especially proud. After spending many hours on this doll, it was a little difficult parting with her. After putting in so much time, they aren't just dolls any longer, but become your pride and joy, your creation, but then sometimes you have to let them go.

Anthony is from Chicago and we met at work. He has a degree in design and used to do some fashion designs for women's clothing. When Anthony first saw the bride doll, he thought she was just beautiful and told me that he would like to do some designing for *BARBIE®* doll fashions. So we pooled our talents together and decided to work together on *BARBIE®* doll designing. At first I was astounded that a man would be interested in doll clothes. We soon became good friends, and we are looking forward to more exciting and different designs in the future."

Tami Bruton

Creations by Tami Bruton

"I have always loved the *BARBIE*® doll. I got my first one when I was three years old and I still have her today. She was the first *Fashion Queen BARBIE*® doll.

Last year, I rediscovered my old *BARBIE*® dolls, many needing repairs and hair and facial makeovers. I have always loved art of any kind, design and crafts, so this was a great challenge. Thus, my newfound career as a fashion doll artist and collector began. I bought Jim Faraone's books and learned a great deal from the "How To" sections. I learned to recondition the hair, cut, curl and restyle it. I also remove all traces of factory facial paint and hand paint the faces to reflect just the right expression. I love to shop and discover the most elegant fabrics for my fashion. Each creation is different and great detail is seen in the facial painting, hair and finishing details of the outfits and jewelry.

I always create one-of-a-kind designs because I choose the fabric first and let my imagination run wild rather than start with a sketch. I have so much fun improvising and adding new things as I go. I get lost in each creation until it is finished and she looks back at me.

These dolls are truly a passion and obsession for me to design and create. There are so many unfinished possibilities. I hope to continue to improve on my creative ideas and share experiences with other artists.

Many thanks to my family, Tom, Jim Faraone, and my many customers for their enthusiasm, their encouragement and their support."

Anne-Marie Burns

Creations by Anne-Marie Burns

"Originally from Glasgow, Scotland, I now live just outside Toronto in Canada. I am also an avid rose grower and admirer.

When I first discovered Mel Odom's *Gene*® doll in 1996, it was in the back of a magazine in a very small advertisement amongst pictures of the *BARBIE*® dolls. For months her face haunted me and then I began calling doll shops in Canada for the *Gene*® doll. I hesitated long enough that the *Premiere Gene*® doll retired, but when I made the drive to pick up my first *Gene*® doll, I was in awe at first sight, as I really did not know what they looked like until I came face to face with the dolls. I came home with *Blue Goddess* and several others. On the way home in the car, I was already redressing them.

Having been on the Internet for some time, I immediately went off in search of the *Gene*® doll on-line. This is where I happened to find the Ashton Drake Forum and Stephen Long's site, which was closing down a week later. Otherwise, the Internet had very little on the *Gene*® doll and no close-up pictures of her details. I began working on a web site for the *Gene*® doll immediately. My photography at this point had mainly been focused on plants and roses, but the *Gene*® doll's movie star quality lent themselves to the first graphics of the *Gene*® doll with close up details for new collectors coming on line. In one year, Anne-Marie's Dolls and Garden received almost 38,000 visitors for the *Gene*® doll-related information and pictures.

In May of 1997, I met Tom Logan through the AD Forum, and his concept of a *Gene*® doll Fan's Couture Showcase developed into reality. The creativity that the *Gene*® doll brought out in collectors required a platform. A web page was built and we encouraged other designers to participate in the monthly showcases. For the next ten months, more and more artists were joining the Showcases and displaying their talents.

By September of that year, I had been approached so often through the Showcases to sell my outfits which were displayed

Billy®'s boyfriend *Carlos*® in Scottish Highland kilt set.

Cissy in a gray Dupioni silk suit - One-of-a-kind.

there that I very nervously opened La Petite Boutique, where everything was *Gene®* doll-size. My sewing over the years had been bridal and avant garde for a boutique in Toronto, and sewing for dolls required a few adjustments, not only in technique but also in my approach. The *Gene®* doll's era is the 40s to 60s, which to me embodies grace, style and femininity. I admire clean lines and simple structure and focus my fashions on opulent and sumptuous fabrics. Color, weight and textures are very important to me and my designs make use of imported fabrics from France and Germany. Much consideration goes into the fabric pattern, which must be in doll scale as well as the garnishments and accessories. Mary Beyer of Arizona, whose couture for dolls is unfailing in good taste, style and quality, was a major influence on me and I remain her fan and admirer to this day.

I have also expanded to the *Cissy®* doll, the *Coco®* doll, the *Miss Revlon®* doll, the *Dollikins®* dolls, Franklin Mint's® *Diana*, *Jackie* and *Marilyn* dolls and couture for the Robert Tonner *American Models®* dolls and *Julia®* doll, which has encouraged collectors to re-dress and play with these dolls. La Petite Boutique is now a shop for fashionable dolls.

In January 1999, The Vogue Collection was first offered. This collection is an exclusive line of Chanel-inspired customized and re-dressed *Gene®* dolls available only through Vogue Collectibles in Oshawa, Canada.

What began as a hobby grew to a part time job and then a full time career for me. My work schedule for the boutique is 14 hours, 6 days a week. The seventh day is for shopping for supplies and sending out packages. Having worked in the corporate world for 23 years prior to dedicating myself full time to the boutique, I can honestly say I thoroughly enjoy every moment at La Petite Boutique."

Gillian in a plaid wool coat dress.

Franklin Mint *Marilyn Monroe* in leopard dress.

Diane Carino

Creations by Diane Carino

"My name is Diane Carino and I live in a suburb near Chicago, Illinois. I'm a chemical engineer by degree. DLC Creations started as a fun hobby but soon changed to a small business in 1994. I basically sew clothes for fashion dolls, but also make jewelry and sometimes, when I feel inspired, I'll customize a doll or two. I like creating a little bit of everything from evening gowns, historical costumes and masquerades costume to fairies and angels. I also like to make sure my outfits are one-of-a-kind. Occasionally, I'll copy a previous design, but I usually make sure it's not exactly alike by changing the color or using a different fabric. To me, each outfit is like an individual work of art and should be distinctive. My interest in creating different outfits must come from my eclectic interests in movies, television, books, antiques, jewelry and music. I believe there is inspiration everywhere from colors and fabrics to movies and music.

I can't really explain why I create a particular outfit. Sometimes a movie or a book inspires me, and I'm constantly looking for ideas and pictures of outfits I could possibly make for dolls. Since I read historical romances, I love to create historical costumes. In fact, romance books are what started my interest in historical fashions. Fabric is also a good source of inspiration. No matter what I do, I cannot resist the temptation of going into a fabric store and looking for fabric that is doll scale. I will come out with several pieces of fabric with the sales clerk always asking me what I'm doing with all the ½-yard pieces of fabric. I usually say I'm making doll clothes, when in actuality, I'm hoarding fabric. I have more fabric now that I make doll clothes than I ever did when I made people clothes.

All of the outfits I make are from patterns I have created, and I could never imagine sewing without a pattern. Creating a pattern is a serious engineering endeavor. Everything has to be perfectly measured to the last fraction of an inch. I measure my subjects carefully and draw out patterns that would make any engineer proud. At first my designs were fairly simple but as I became a more experienced seamstress, my designs and patterns became more elaborate and complex and took longer to complete. I pride myself on details like lining jackets and bodices, sewing loops for working buttons on shirts, and patterns perfectly tailored to that distinctive fashion doll figure. To me it's important that a doll's outfit be as detailed and accurate as a real person's outfit. Playability is also an important aspect of my designs. I make sure all my edges are finished and that all pieces are easy to remove and

put on. My philosophy is dolls that are for playing; therefore, they must have clothes that can be put on and taken off.

What does the future hold for DCL Creations? Since I only do one show a year, I like to feature different types of designs. My latest project is creating a line of dolls called 'Femme Fatales.' These dolls will be dressed in provocative leather and vinyl outfits with special accessories to match their personalities. I have also branched out to creating outfits for larger fashion dolls because I can use up my fabric hoard faster and it's just plain easier sewing for larger dolls. At a doll show, it usually takes people some time to find me because they can never figure out what I'll have at my table. What is important to me is that my creations go home to people who appreciate them. So if you happen to be at the Joe and Marl Show in Chicago, drop in and say, 'Hi.'"

Karen Cooper

Creations by Karen Cooper

"My name is Karen Cooper and I currently live in Cordova, Tennessee. I grew up in Southern California and have lived at West Point, New York and in Austin, Texas.

My renewed interest in fashion dolls started about a year and a half ago. I was shopping and saw a doll that resembled me, and that one doll started it all. I soon restyled her hair and started making her clothes. My mother had always sewn for my *BARBIE*® dolls, so I thought it would be fun to do the same.

Not too long after that I discovered *Barbie Bazaar*® magazine. Inside was an advertisement for Ninimomo Creations. I could not believe my eyes, as this was my first exposure to exquisite customized dolls. I became consumed with how the dolls were produced and began looking for customizing information and tips.

I found Jim's first book and the rest, as they say, is history. Immediately I began doing repaints, as I have an art background and thought this would be fun. I found I enjoyed the intricate detail and the symmetrical challenge. Reroots came next, and I found I could take totally trashed dolls and make them wonderful again. About that time I found the Austin Fashion Doll Club. This is a wonderful group that has provided me with inspiration and encouragement.

As a child I did hundreds of fashion designs. It's funny, but it was only recently that I made the connection. I have always loved designing gowns; unfortunately making them for myself is expensive and not too practical. Designing for fashion dolls gives me the creative outlet and a fun product. Hopefully you'll enjoy the pictures here and on my web site.

For those of you just getting started in customizing (like I've been doing it for so long!) I encourage you to continue, read books like this one, and ask questions. There are groups of customizers on the Internet who communicate regularly. I find this a wonderful resource as the members have different tastes and ways of doing things. Just because you think you can't sew or paint doesn't mean you never will. Passion for what you're doing is the minimum requirement!"

Patricia Cronin

Creations by Patricia Cronin
Photos by Pat Henry

"From childhood into adulthood, I have always enjoyed miniatures. When I was a little girl I used to make miniature saddles for my horse statues, ultimately working all the way down to an entire collection of saddles and stable tools for my favorite 2½-inch horse. My fascination for 'tiny things' only grew as time passed.

I studied fine arts at Skidmore College but left after a year and eventually moved on to obtaining my degree in performing arts at Virginia Commonwealth University. After graduating from college, I felt I was ready for the 'Big Time,' so I formed a rock band and started singing in clubs. We would rehearse in my basement surrounded by all of my 'junk art.' I had an antique button collection and fabrics to make band costumes, a welding torch for making jewelry, canvases, paints, and last, but not least, my trusty little featherweight Singer sewing machine. I left most of that stuff behind when I moved to New York. (Nowhere to put it!) Fortunately, I always kept that featherweight!

While singing in New York at night and working for Bergdorf Goodman by day, my love of fashion was rekindled. I was able to appreciate first-hand the craftsmanship and technique of the top designers like Yves St. Laurent, Versace, and Karl Lagerfeld, among others. I also discovered FAO right across the street!

I was soon hooked on the chic Mdvanii fashions in the doll department, and my first 'mini-mannequin' purchase was a secondary-market *Feelin' Groovy*® doll by Billy Boy® (What a babe!). Soon followed the *Gene*® doll, and the rest, as they say, is history! I was totally hooked!

I now search all over the country for antique beads, vintage flowers, and rare fabrics. I'm always looking for a lead on something unique and beautiful to use in a creation. For each design, the framework for my concept always starts with the same basic elements: drama, fantasy, wonder and elegance. Occasionally, to fulfill a concept I collaborate with the superb doll craftsmen, repainter Ken Bartram and rerooter Tommy DeMaria. Working together with others is the greatest of fun!

My reward in this is the tremendous amount of satisfaction I get from the creation of a design and from the responses I get from the people who own my work."

Midnight Blues

Shall We Dance

Walking Fifi

The Sorceress

Georgia Doyle

Creations by Georgia Doyle

"I was born in Waco, Texas in January of 1962. My mom was a homemaker and my dad was an artist and chemist. I've always loved to draw and design, and at the early age of seven, I was already taking pieces of material to use as gowns for my fashion dolls. We didn't buy many 'real' outfits, so I used my imagination to create lavish gowns held on my dolls with rubber bands and straight pins! In my child's eye they were the most beautiful creations a girl could want!

At around 10 years old I became fascinated with faces. I began collecting pictures of celebrities when I was 13, and started copying those faces into pencil drawings. Since my dad was an artist he helped me to develop my technique and about a year later he determined that I was experienced enough to begin painting in oils. He taught me how to add shading and light to capture the attention of the observer.

I most enjoyed painting glamorous people, which is why I originally concentrated on celebrities. When I found out about the limitations of copyright laws, I became very frustrated and put aside my art.

Then I began collecting vintage fashion dolls. In 1995, I sent my friend Ann Meili an E-mail with pictures of my paintings. She really liked my work and suggested that I create a celebrity look-a-like fashion doll. So I set out to create my first masterpiece! Since I use fashion dolls, my celebrities are not exactly like the person I'm painting, but are close enough that people recognize who it is supposed to be without violating copyright laws.

I started by just re-painting the dolls' faces. When collectors saw my work and liked it, I decided to create the entire doll. I began by hand sewing the doll clothes because I was a bit intimidated by the sewing machine. I draped the material on the doll (as I had done as a child) and pinned it into position. Then I turned it inside out and sewed it together. I soon discovered that I could design outfits without using a pre-cut pattern. I occasionally use patterns, but when I am not limited to a pattern, my imagination is able to soar! I also overcame my fear of the sewing machine!

I now paint some of my doll creations onto canvas in oils. I believe that God guides our destiny, and if you are patient, He will guide you to use your talents in the best way you can. I hope you enjoy looking at my creations. E-mail me and let me know what you think. I would love to hear from you."

Marilyn
(Jewelry by
Thomas
Originals)

GEORGIA DOYLE
3110 Cascade Ave
Pueblo, CO 81008
E-mail: dollpainter@yahoo.com
Web Site:
http://www.geocities.com/FashionAvenue/Stage/2635/index.html

Geisha (Kimono by
Thomas Originals)

Snow Leopard and Tiger

Joanne Ellem

Creations by Joanne Ellem

"An exotic childhood full of color has led me to a life in the pursuit of color. I always felt that I would be either a fashion designer or a movie star, and after experiencing life and traveling, I finally decided to enter the world of the absolutely fabulous and become a fashion designer (with the intention that the movie star thing would come later). My love for the unusual and a healthy diet of Japanese animation while growing up made my connection with Takara's *Jenny*® doll a foregone conclusion. I have found the perfect clothes horse to be a beautiful doll. Unlike many teachers, models and clients, this lady doesn't complain and always seems happy about the clothes!

Coming from a background of administration and accounting and now at the point of almost completing a bachelor of design, I can dress my favorite plastic lady in individually designed clothes made specifically for the *Jenny*® doll and all her friends. Specializing in one-of-a-kind dolls and clothes, with the eventual inclusion of hand crafted, furniture pieces and Art Nouveau-style dress makers stands (by craftswoman Kate Holt), I will soon be appearing on the pages of the World Wide Web."

JOANNE ELLEM
1/78 Murray Farm Rd.
Beecroft, NSW 2119
Australia
E-mail: jobrent@magna.com.au

Janine Faini

"I have always loved *BARBIE*® dolls, but my first doll was a *Casey*® doll. I really loved her and made fashions for her. My first attempt at creating my own fashions began early, around age four. My first outfit was a washcloth and tape dress, very stylish. I have come a long way since then! Unfortunately, during junior high and high school I packed my dolls away and never gave them a second thought. It was not until my junior year in college that I rediscovered the *BARBIE*® doll. I was browsing in a bookstore when I saw the 1985 blue Manos book. As I was looking through the pages, I saw my dolls there. Unfortunately, mine were not mint, as they had been played with, but I loved them anyway! My first purchase that year was the *My First BARBIE*® *Doll* and, as they say, the rest is history.

It was not until 1988 that I started creating my own fashions for the *BARBIE*® doll and her friends, as well as costumes from movies. Now I make a little bit of everything from ice skating costumes to coats and even dabble in rerooting hair. Some of my favorite outfits to make are movie costumes, Princess Diana fashions, and cheerleading outfits. I used to make many cheerleading outfits from different schools, but now I focus on the University of Notre Dame since I live thirty minutes away from campus and when I go to games I can take pictures of the outfits. I also make Indiana University cheerleading outfits because that's the school where I graduated. I had to

Creations by Janine Faini

include my Alma Mater! I enjoy working with all kinds of materials and accessories and am always experimenting. I am also a perfectionist, so the outfit you see today may be different tomorrow. I have been known to redo an outfit over as many as four times until it's perfect! Needless to say, I really love creating fashions!"

Kristi Yamaguchi

Skipper fashions.

Princess Diana circa 1996-97.

JANINE FAINI
P.O. Box 1292
Mishawaka, IN 46544
E-mail: JAFNice@aol.com

Dorothy Fannin

Creations by Dorothy Fannin
Photos by Bill B. Fannin

"I am very new at customizing fashion dolls, not starting until 1998 when I discovered Jim Faraone's first book, *Fashion Doll Makeovers*. I was immediately attracted to the creations of Kayandem. With a gentle shove from my friend, Imelda Sanchez, a fellow fashion doll artist who shares my "Living Dolls" web site, I was spurred into making molded hair dolls of my own.

I was born in Washington, D.C. during the Depression, and didn't have any dolls to play with except the paper dolls my mother found for me in *McCall's* magazine. I would sit and play with them for hours. I had an average upbringing, going to school in Washington, D.C. and in Maryland and working as a soda jerk, telephone operator and dental assistant before getting married.

In 1956, I moved with my husband and our family to Tucson, Arizona, where I still live. I am the mother of three children, the grandmother of two and am expecting a great grandchild in September 1999.

Over the years I've attended art classes at the University of Arizona and photography classes at the Tucson Museum of Art. My photographs have been published in three books, several booklets and in *Darkroom Photography* magazine.

If anyone had told me when I was younger that I would be playing with dolls at my age, I would probably have laughed at them. My interest in collecting dolls really didn't even begin until 1980, when my granddaughter was born. We now have an extensive collection of fashion dolls and a wonderful assortment of customized dolls from friends I've met on the net.

Since, after my cataract surgery, I can no longer sew like I used to, many of my dolls have been glamorized by the fashions of Norma Pallanes of Tucson and Anita Ramirez of Tijuana, Mexico. The sparkle in my dolls' eyes comes from the brushes of Imelda Sanchez, who also taught me how to make jewelry. I am currently working at creating feather fashions, a process I find both fascinating and challenging.

I still have so much more to learn about customizing and am hoping to "keep on, keeping on" experimenting with my molded hair dolls for as long as I can. I hope you like my dolls as much as I have enjoyed making them."

DOROTHY FANNIN
Living Dolls
5731 E. 7th St.
Tucson, AZ 85711
E-mail: dfannin@azstarnet.com
Web Site: http://www.azstarnet.com/~dfannin

Mike Franklin

Creations by Mike Franklin

"I believe my love for fashion dolls began in 1962 when, at the age of 4, I watched as my sister's brunette bubble cut *BARBIE®* doll and flocked-haired *Ken®* doll came into the house. I had never given any of her other baby dolls a second look, but these 'miniature adults' fascinated me. I wasn't happy until I had an identical pair of my own. After a year or so, I remember giving them away to a little girl whose family couldn't afford to buy her a *BARBIE®* doll. It made her very happy, but as soon as they went out the door, I immediately regretted it. I guess I put it out of my mind and pretty much ignored the existence of fashion dolls until I rediscovered the *BARBIE®* doll at the age of 35.

With memories of high quality vintage dolls and clothes in my head, I realized I wasn't happy with most of the modern products I saw on the store shelves. Then I saw them...photos of the custom, one-of-a-kind dolls created by the likes of MíKelman and Ivan Burton. 'This is what I want!' I proclaimed, and since I couldn't afford to buy their creations, I decided that the only way I was going to have dolls and fashions like these was to try making them myself. I bought a sewing machine, paint and brushes, and a few low-priced dolls to experiment with. Most of my first attempts were pretty embarrassing, but I knew that if I kept at it, I'd get better. It's been a painfully slow process with lots of frustration along the way. When it comes to my sewing abilities, I feel that I still have lots to learn, but at least now I have more successes than failures with my attempts at 'couture.' One rule for doll clothing that I've tried to adopt from

Satin Soiree

Real Men

the artists I most admire is making sure the clothing fits properly and conforms to the doll's every curve. It's one element that can make or break the entire look of the doll.

These days, I enjoy collecting and customizing a wide range of fashion dolls.... the *BARBIE®* doll, the *Candi®* doll, the *Charisse®* doll, the *Gene®* doll, the *Julia®* doll...there are a lot of great dolls available today to choose from. Each has its own distinct charms and personality, and more new and different ones are showing up on a steady basis. I've only been attempting to sell my creations for a short time. I'm very happy that so far, a lot of people seem to enjoy my work, and that I've been fairly successful at doing something that's so much fun! One of my biggest thrills was that the very first doll I ever sold... 'Satin Soiree' was purchased by one of the nation's leading fashion doll experts, Joe Blitman.

I have to give most of the credit to the artists whose work first inspired me to try my hand at it and gave me the inspiration to keep learning and growing as I try to make the quality and style of each new project surpass the last one. Working at a full-time "real" job doesn't allow me to spend as much time on projects as I'd like. It seems that I'm not able to create a new doll or outfit very often these days, but every moment I can spend working with fashion dolls is always the most enjoyable part of the day.

Anyone interested in viewing my latest projects can see them on my web site."

Spotting Bargains

Royal Reception

Rose Royale

Dennis Foster Greco

Creations by Dennis Foster Greco

"I am a native of Brooklyn, New York, a hair stylist and a fashion designer. I made my first artist doll on a dare from a friend who is an avid *BARBIE*® doll collector. Commenting that some of the dolls I had seen had flaws in keeping the proportions of accessories to size, I set out to find all the right items for my dolls. That first doll was such a success that friends of my friend wanted dolls for themselves. Thus, "D. Foster Creations", my doll business, was established.

Since my first professional show for the "1st World of Collectibles" at Atlantic City, New Jersey in April 1995, I have been very active in all the local shows in the New England area. I have done shows for Blue Ribbon Productions, F&M Promotions, JMK Shows, Joe and Marl Shows and Kitty's Collectibles to name a few, and was a participant at the 1997 San Diego Convention and the 1998 Atlanta Convention.

While I started with hand knits, I have also worked with silk flowers, lace fringe and most lately with suede, leather and feathers.

In the fall of '98 I started to get involved with the *Gene*® doll and have found it to be very gratifying and successful.

In the last four years, there are a few things that have not changed, and one is my commitment to use the best quality. I continue to use only 14 karat gold jewelry and semi-precious stones to finish my dolls. I still maintain my one-of-a-kind only policy and will not repeat the same dress on any doll. The dolls are always photographed front and back after they are finished and all details noted.

Ladies who have stopped at the display always comment that the dolls are better dressed, coifed and jeweled than they are. I still reply that 'nothing is too good for the *BARBIE*® doll.'

I still have the same two people working with me as in the beginning: Linda Ignatow on hair and Teak Lewis on gowns. Either one or both of them will be found with me at a show.

I had the good fortune to have my dolls featured in the Artist Showcase of the summer 1997 issue of *MILLER'S*® magazine."

D. FOSTER CREATIONS
P.O. Box 666
Smallwood, N.Y. 12778
(914) 583-7317

David Howard

Creations by David Howard

"I have been collecting and customizing all types of toys since I was a kid. I even carved my own Star Wars® figures out of wood and painted them before plastic figures ever hit my hometown of Corsicana, Texas, back in 1977. When I graduated from college I got my mom to drag out all of my old *G.I. Joe®* dolls and I was hooked once again. I got involved with the *BARBIE®* doll when my wife, Angie, rediscovered her childhood dolls five years ago. She and I now collect *BARBIE®* dolls and *G.I. Joe®* dolls together and she considers me her 'technical consultant.'

Last year after attending a convention in Atlanta, my wife urged me to give customizing the *BARBIE®* doll a try for a local *BARBIE®* doll club meeting. I had been customizing the *G.I. Joe®* dolls for quite a while and thought, 'What the heck, I can do this.' I created a doll for the Halloween contest at our local *BARBIE®* doll club meeting. I won second place and was very excited about it.

I am a creative director for a Dallas advertising agency, so being creative kind of came naturally, but I had never really considered applying it to the hobby of *BARBIE®* doll collecting. Soon after the local contest I took the 'one-night-stand' *BARBIE®* doll to the Tulsa mini-convention, where she placed first in her category. Jim Faraone was a judge in the competition and asked me if I would consider putting my dolls in his book. Of course I was ecstatic. As you can see, I have continued my custom *BARBIE®* doll outfits and try to create dolls that are very conceptional without focusing so much on fashion. I want people to smile when they see my dolls and I create them purely for fun. I would encourage anyone who collects dolls or action figures to give customizing a try. It has been a very satisfying extension of our hobbies for both me and my wife. I hope you enjoy my creations."

WWI Soldiers

Talk to Me

Color My World

Viva Las Vegas

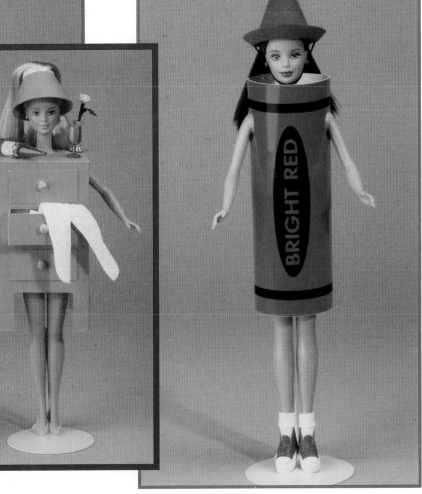

DAVID HOWARD
3106 Birch Dr.
Carrollton, TX 75007

One Night Stand

Cindy Izon

Creations by Cindy Izon

"I started designing *BARBIE* doll clothes when I was eight years old. Of course they weren't nearly as sophisticated as my creations are today! I enjoy it much more now, since I have a car and can drive myself to the store to go poking around for the perfect trim or fabric! Age definitely has its advantages.

Each one of my creations is pure fun to me. When I started My Girl Originals, my sister, Kim Collins, was my partner. We would play with the *BARBIE* doll for eight hours a day and at the end of the day, it would seem like we had just started. There really are no words to express what that wonderful time we spent together means to me. She had to quit in 1997 since her lupus was affecting her kidneys and her health was deteriorating. Prior to that, in 1996 Kim actually started our local *BARBIE* Doll Club in Tulsa. Of course, I was there to back her up and together we made it an enormously fun experience. Our club is still going strong with two mini-conventions under our belt and a national convention coming in 2000. I really enjoyed designing the outfits for the mini-conventions that our club had. The first convention, 'Super Sonic Weekend,' featured the 'Sonic Car Hop Doll' and was particularly fun to create, since I love to eat at the Sonic Drive-In! They have the best burgers and shakes. (I had hoped that Sonic would anoint me their Queen and give me a lifetime supply of food for all my dolly efforts. Oh well!) It was particularly significant that the *BARBIE* doll and Sonic were 'born' in 1959, so of course we used the 35th Anniversary *BARBIE* doll to compliment the theme.

I can honestly say that the 'Moonlight Masquerade Doll' from our second convention was beautiful and the convention was a blast, with everyone coming dressed in costume on Halloween night. Mere words can't accurately describe the scene — a ballroom full of *BARBIE* doll collectors, all in costume!

As for my designs, there is a never-ending flow of color, shape and form rumbling around in my head. Sometimes I know I drive my friends to madness when I call them up and run my ideas by them, but that's what friends are for, right? There is nothing in this world that warms my heart more than when I have made a custom doll for someone and they write or call to tell me that they are so very thrilled because it was just what they wanted. There is no feeling that compares to knowing that you have brought another person joy.

My greatest wish is to be able to free the *BARBIE* doll from the confines of her boxes and to apply my creativity to her world. Life is just too short not to be able to touch and be touched!"

Michael Jankun

Creations by Michael Jankun

"Unlike a lot of male collectors, I never had a toy taken away from me or destroyed when I was a child. My mother had the 'radical' idea that her four children should be encouraged to play together and to share their toys. As a result, it wasn't unusual for my older brother's *G.I. Joes*® to 'date' my older sister's *BARBIE*® dolls, or for my younger sister's *Skipper*® dolls to hang out with my *Steve Scout*® figures.

At collector shows and conventions, I like to identify myself as a Bostonian by wearing shirts of the various Boston area sports teams. In spite of that quirk, I have never been much of an athlete. As a child, I preferred to read, draw and play with my Legos® and my action figures. I had many of the action figures that were popular during the 70s: the *Big Jim*® doll, the *Steve Scout*® doll, the *Bionic Man*® doll, Star Wars® figures and the Mego® super heroes. I never actually gave up most of the toys, so I can't really state an age at which I started collecting.

Even as a child, I was frustrated by the lack of female action figures. (What does Superman do if he doesn't have Lois Lane to rescue?) As an adult, I began to buy a few fashion dolls in order to make up for the lack of females in my collection. I was also becoming less interested in new action figure lines. Even the *G.I. Joe*® figure had been shrunken down to four inches in height. I began to realize that I preferred the open-ended nature of the male and female fashion dolls, and I began to haunt doll shows, digging through bargain bins in search of new acquisitions.

Eventually, I met people who shared my interests, and I became a member of a club now known as the Collectors of New England. Through the club, I became interested in the national *BARBIE*® doll collectors' conventions, and in 1992, I attended the convention in Niagara Falls. Like a lot of attendees, I was fascinated by the handmade creations entered in the convention's competition. However, I also thought, 'I could do that.' Before long, I was making plans for the 1993 convention in Baltimore.

I had minimal sewing skills, but, over the course of a year, I taught myself the basics of patterns, darts, hems and the use of a sewing machine. The hard work paid off. In Baltimore I won four ribbons, including first place and best in show for my hand-made King Arthur chess set. Since then, I have attended several conventions and won quite a few ribbons. My entries range from a single Samurai warrior to thirteen dolls representing the signs of the zodiac. I've done historical figures, ballet dancers, Broadway performers, sci-fi aliens and comic book super heroes. About half of my work has focused on male characters, which is very unusual in a hobby filled with female dolls in fluffy ball gowns. Naturally, I wish that there were more male fashion dolls. There are a wide variety of female dolls on the market, but it's nearly impossible to find an Asian or Hispanic male doll, or even a blonde or redhead.

Although I have made items for raffles and conventions, I am not yet comfortable with the idea of selling my creations. My chief advice to other potential doll artists is to trust your own creativity, learn what you can, don't fear mistakes and have fun!"

The Martian Spy Girl from "Mars Attacks" (Belle doll)

Chess set from Baltimore convention

Brad Jensen

Creations by Brad Jensen

"As a child, dolls were my companions, friends and entertainment. I knew that as I became older I was 'supposed' to grow out of dolls, so in 1984 I sold my *BARBIE®* doll wardrobe that I'd made from scraps along with my favorite doll at the time, the *Beauty Secrets BARBIE®* doll.

I've always had a broad spectrum of interests. I entered college as an architecture student and later became a cosmetologist!

I became acquainted with the *BARBIE®* doll and other fashion dolls in 1996 when I wanted to make a Catwoman doll. With a 'bend and move' *BARBIE®* doll body, a good understanding of patterns and some black neoprene I began my project. Even though in the end, her gunboat feet ruined the effect of an otherwise wonderful costume, I was hooked.

Fashion dolls are all about fantasy and I like to express that in my designs. I enjoy Bob Mackie's designs more than any other. His designs often cross the line between fashion and costume. I appreciate and admire his flair for fantasy. I like to challenge myself with each new design. Attention to small details such as capturing just the right facial expression with paint or hiding tiny zippers all help to create the overall effect that make the design experience rewarding and satisfying."

BRAD JENSEN CREATIONS
Brad Jensen
4554 N. 50th Dr.
Phoenix, AZ 85031
E-mail: brad@bradjensen.com
Web Site: http://www.bradjensen.com

Warrior Woman

Callisto

Nancy Kella

Creations by Nancy Kella
Photos by Lori Kella

"I don't remember a time in my life when I wasn't designing and sewing. Even at the young age of five I was making clothes for my dolls. As a matter of fact, I don't remember learning to sew; it just seemed to come naturally to me. Since my grandmother was a tailor and my mother a seamstress, I'm sure my talent was inherited and for that I am very grateful.

I've also been collecting dolls since I was a child and will always remember when the *BARBIE®* doll was added to my collection. I'd always loved dolls, but from the moment I saw the *BARBIE®* doll a year earlier I was absolutely hooked. I just loved the doll booklets and marveled at all the little accessories.

I was never able to have any of the 'store bought' fashions, so I was always making clothes and accessories for my doll. I still have all my dolls and clothes and even have the first hat box I made. I also made doll clothes for my two younger sisters. By the time I was in high school I was not only making all my own clothes, but was also making and selling clothes for the *BARBIE®* dolls. I even took my *BARBIE®* dolls to college with me and continued to make and sell clothes for them.

I have a BS degree in medical technology from Western Michigan University. While that was a rewarding profession, my heart was always into sewing and designing and I continued to do so in my spare time. Fortunately, I had two daughters who I could sew for, making fashions for them and their dolls. I was also able to continue adding to my doll collection, buying pink box dolls for myself as I purchased them for my daughters.

It wasn't until a few years ago, with both my children in college, that I finally had time to design for my own dolls again. At about the same time my husband was transferred from Cleveland, Ohio, to Asheville, North Carolina. That's when I decided it was time for a change in my life. Instead of going back to work, I started to concentrate on the things I loved most and Designs by Nancy was the result. I've been very busy ever since and love every minute of it.

At first I sold just my outfits at shows. Because I didn't always like the 'look' of the outfits on the dolls and wanted more color in their faces, I taught myself how to repaint faces and restyle hair. I also learned to reroot hair and eyelashes. When I took my finished display dolls to shows, people always wanted to buy them. I finally gave in and now I sell both finished and separate outfits.

DESIGNS BY NANCY
Nancy Kella
301 Jennifer Lane
Asheville, NC 28803
E-mail: nkella@aol.com
Web Site: http://user.talstar.com/dbn

Citrus Fun

My clothes are made from quality fabrics like silk and ultrasuede and have fine details such as hand sewn hems and linings. Because of my love of color, many of my dolls have brightly colored outfits. I also love making all the little accessories like hats, purses, gloves, hose and jewelry that complete each design. All the clothes are removable with hand sewn snaps or buttons.

I don't have time to attend many doll shows anymore. I have my own web site and have been very busy just trying to keep up with that. I've had many good responses to my creations and am very pleased that so many people enjoy them.

I would like to give a special thanks to my daughter Lori for putting her photography degree to good use and photographing my dolls for this feature."

Business Appointment

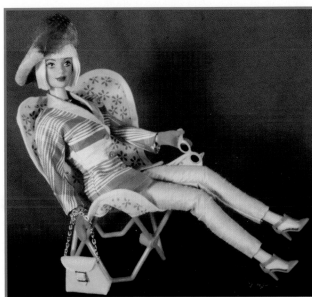

Trendsetter

Animal Instinct

High Style

Elizabeth Lee

Creations by Elizabeth Lee

"My name is Liz, I'm English, I live in London and I just adore fashion dolls. I have been collecting for about four years, and most of my collection is either vintage or bizarre!

I started customizing about 18 months ago, as I was tired of the vapid looks on most modern dolls' faces and wanted something stronger, more powerful. I decided that I wanted to do something different and experimented with a variety of mediums to get the effect I wanted. I was looking for the extreme and unusual and felt that I had only started on the path I wanted to follow.

I get my inspiration from all manner of places - the sea, nature, cityscapes, patterns of light and shade, traditional sources like paintings and books and even computer games. At the moment I am working with a lot of natural themes, having noticed the beautiful colors of winter landscapes in England. I have always been very interested in folk costumes and look to them for ideas of embroidery and decoration.

I do not want my dolls to look immaculate — the wilder the better — I do not try for perfectly coifed hair — I want it to look as if she has just climbed out of the forest or woken up from the flowers. I do not aim for my dolls to look realistic - I am aiming for a fantastic, almost fairy-like look on some, and a semi-robotic look on others...someone once referred to my dolls as Inter Galactic Space Witches!

Most of all I enjoy painting. Once I start I can go on forever, and I would love to be able to spend more time each week on my craft. I love to change the expression on a face, or better, get a doll with rubbed face paint and make her look beautiful again. When I started customizing I wanted to work only on the junk shop dolls, but I could not resist the beautiful face molds on some of the new dolls. My favorite model is the closed mouth (Mackie) *BARBIE®* doll, but I also love the Diva mold found on the modern *Midge®* doll. Although I do work on other dolls, I prefer the *BARBIE®* doll, the *Teresa®* doll and the *Midge®* doll above all others.

Not being overly fond of sewing, I look for alternative methods of clothing for my dolls, although tying a piece of fabric to get the desired look can take me

ELIZABETH LEE
Re: Vamp
17, Rosemont Rd.
Acton, London W3 9LU
England
(0) 181-932-1898
E-mail: wdl@nipcus.co.uk

quite some time, so I am thinking about starting to sew. I have done a few dressed dolls, but find it a little restrictive.

One of my main problems, which I am sure is the same for almost everyone in this book, is that I never seem to have enough time to work with my dolls. At the time of writing I am president of the *BARBIE®* doll Collectors Club of Great Britain, and also work full time as a teacher of English as a foreign language, a job which has taken me all over the world. I am married, and my husband displays remarkable tolerance. He gives me lots of encouragement in my customizing, and offers plenty of ideas, constructive criticism and praise!

In the future, I want to further develop my painting techniques — I confess I find eyebrows very hard to do and I want to do more work on the repositioning of arms and fingers, which is the greatest fun!

Some of my non-collecting friends feel very sorry for my dolls. After I had brought in a new supply of Florida *BARBIE®* dolls, a friend looked at them and commented, 'Look at them sitting there, smiling in their swimsuits...They don't know what you are going to do to them yet - all the boiling.' 'Well,' I replied, 'It is necessary to suffer to be beautiful...'"

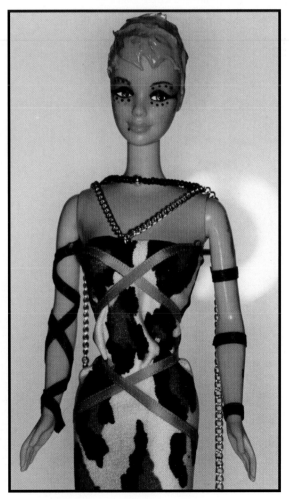

Travis Manning

Creations by Travis Manning

"I started collecting dolls in 1988 and before I knew it, I had hundreds of dolls that weren't really that unusual. I was becoming bored with the hobby, so I started doing some customizing in 1990, creating a technique to 'mold' hairs on my dolls. My favorite dolls to work on are ethnic dolls (Mattel's *Shani*® dolls, *Asha*® dolls and *Nichelle*® dolls are my favorite!) and male dolls, giving them more 'trendy' looks than most manufacturers would. I also enjoy flocking hair on dolls. I have tried to fine-tune my facial painting techniques over the years, and they've definitely improved with time. I do know my limits, and am not very talented when it comes to sewing costumes for dolls. For the most part, I use existing costumes and just alter the doll's hair and facial painting and sometimes mix and match to create an individualized look.

I live in central Illinois with my partner of eight years and we have a very active four-year-old Dalmatian. I work as a beauty operator and spend most of my spare time exercising, drawing and being outdoors. I am also an avid collector of Cruella De Vil items and 'collect' Doc Marten shoes and boots as well."

1998 Travis and Mike

TRAVIS MANNING
708 E. Fremont St.
Bloomington, IL 61701
E-mail: Ashaholic@aol.com

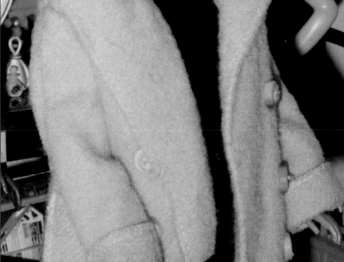

Kraig McLaughlin

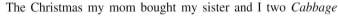

Creations by Kraig McLaughlin
Photos by Gilles Toucas

"I've collected toys all my life. As a kid, I thought the ultimate job was to be a toy designer. Growing up in the 80s, I was fascinated with Xavier Roberts and his *Cabbage Patch Kid*® dolls. I thought, 'That's what I want! My own doll!'

I have always been crafty, and at an early age learned to sew from my father and grandmother. The Christmas my mom bought my sister and I two *Cabbage Patch Kid*® dolls each, however, I became inspired. I took a shot at creating my own soft sculpture dolls. A local craft store had everything I needed and I studied other dolls and experimented. The pattern my Mom bought me wasn't quite right, so I made my own. I did the hair, the facial paint, and the 'sculpting.' The clothes came from a local shop, and I named my creations 'K-Kids.' I was pretty proud of myself – I was only ten. My parents even let me have a booth at a local craft show a few times.

A few years later I was honing my sewing skills making costumes for the dance studio where I studied. The soft sculpture craze had died down and dancing became my true passion. I trained until I could finally move to Hollywood and become a professional dancer. In Los Angeles I started making clothes and dance costumes again for my friends. This led to a design job with a growing dancewear company.

My toy design and collecting bug remained dormant for a

few years until an old, well-loved *BARBIE*® doll caught my eye at a thrift store. I had never grown up around fashion dolls, but something just clicked. I took her home and played. I decided to recreate, in miniature, the dance costumes I was making as a way to catalog my designs. I took a trip to the local toy store and fell in love again. I had rediscovered that magical feeling I knew as a kid. I bought a few dolls to redress and haven't stopped since. In 1994 this hobby became an obsession with the Nostalgic Reproduction Series. Now I have hundreds of dolls in my collection and many more waiting to be revamped. I love the early *BARBIE*® doll era and this reflects in my work. When the *Gene*® doll was introduced in 1995, I was floored. Doll collecting and design had been taken to new heights.

I currently work as a dancer/actor in Los Angeles and have a growing costume business. I love designing for the *BARBIE*® doll, the *Gene*® doll and other fashion dolls. I am influenced by vintage fashions both from the doll world and the 'real world.' Pop culture also offers many exciting possibilities and options. Every day I discover new techniques or think of new ideas I can't wait to try. My designs are always evolving. I feel very lucky to be able to transform my hobby, something I truly love, into my livelihood, and to share my love of fashion dolls with others.

It is great to see so many enjoying a rewarding hobby like doll collecting. I have to thank all the other talented artists in this book, and previous books, for inspiring me to keep it up. We feed off each other's energy, offering inspiration and making us stronger."

KRAIG MCLAUGHLIN
5315 Bellingham Ave.
Valley Village, CA 91607
E-mail: KraigMc@aol.com

Karen McGuire

Creations by Karen McGuire

"I'm a second-generation artist - daughter of two artists. My mother was a fine oil painter and watercolorist, then became a fashion designer in New York City working under Oleg Cassini. My father was an executive commercial art director for many years on 5th Avenue in New York City, working for a crewel work design firm.

I had won many awards as a child artist, but went on to the dramatic arts in later childhood and into my twenties. Studying and performing in Greenwich Village, my acting career took a swift turn to writing plays, which I had been doing since I was about seven years old. Having had four comedies produced off-Broadway, I decided to try my skills on the West Coast and shifted to screenplay writing and took some film acting courses as well. Not crazy about the Hollywood scene, I decided to leave California, bought a house in Nevada and settled there for the time being - making over 11½ inch dolls!

I had been collecting fashion dolls, but never thought of making them over until I discovered a little doll shop in Nevada. This shop specialized in collector *BARBIE*® dolls and a friend of the owner was occasionally submitting what she called 'prototypes' to the store on consignment. He showed me a doll called 'Elvira'

which was obviously a Mattel® *Kira*® doll, and he had it up for auction on the Internet. Keeping it all to myself, I thought, 'I can do that!' And I rushed home to try it. A new and exciting talent/hobby was born in me!

I became fascinated with the seemingly unlimited creative powers of the fashion doll makeover artist. I'd seen it on the *BARBIE*® doll TV specials and then in Jim Faraone's books, but when I spoke to others who were uninformed about this art, they looked at me like I had three heads! I had to spread the word. So I started a web site devoted to the promotion of the fashion doll makeover artist. It bloomed into a much larger web site as I added designers of fashions, jewelry, furniture and other accessories, all lovingly created for the fabulous fashion doll. It is quite a challenge keeping this web site maintained, but I love it!

Enjoy my collection, as I do! You can see my work and so many other wonderfully creative fashion doll makeover artists from around the world at designerdolls.com."

Candi® doll as "Agatha Dish, Dolly Detective"

"Fabio"

Ross Miller/Robin Betts

Creations by
Ross Miller/Robin Betts

"Who are MRD?

Masterton Robin Designs are Robin Betts and Ross Miller. We are based in Islington, London, UK. The business started in 1996."

"I (Robin) am a costume designer by profession, working mostly in the area of television and music videos, both in Europe and the USA. I started customizing the *BARBIE®* doll and similar dolls as an extension of this work, partly as a way of trying out ideas and also, sometimes, to give the "star" a miniature copy of the costume. I am responsible for all aspects of the design of the dolls' costumes, hair and our specially commissioned display boxes."

"I (Ross) am an insurance underwriter by profession and still work full time for a specialist insurance company at Canary Wharf in London's Docklands. My hobbies include model making and more recently photography. These have been put to good use as I make all the sets used in the photographs, customize doll bodies as required, repaint the faces, make all the jewelry and am responsible for the financial side of the business."

"Our aim for our first series of dolls 'Hollywood Dreams' is to present an interpretation of the costumes from some of our favorite Hollywood movies (of which we have a huge library). We will never make absolute copies, as these have already been created by the original movie designer —- that just wouldn't be art.

We are also producing a series of one of or very limited designs called 'Hollywood Couture.' These feature not only film-related costumes but also our own couture and showgirl costumes.

We always look out for new creations from other doll artists particularly fellow British doll artists Denise Poole, Franklin Lim Liao, whose creations always inspire us, and Dick Tahsin.

Finally, we are always prepared to consider commissions based on any of the commonly available fashion dolls."

Sally Bowles

Sally Bowles

Jennifer Moffatt

Creations by Jennifer Moffatt

"I love dolls. When I was a little girl, my favorite doll was a TNT *Francie®* doll with long brown hair and brown eyes like me and an outfit that I adored called 'Summer Frost,' which eventually became the name of my company. One of the worst moments in my life was when I became a teenager and was told that I was too old to play with dolls anymore. I had to give up my *Francie®* doll, *BARBIE®* doll, and their friends. All of the clothes I had used my allowance to buy and the ones that I had made while learning to sew had to be packed away. We moved from San Francisco to Las Vegas, and my dolls were left behind with another little girl.

I didn't own another fashion doll for almost 20 years. In between the loss of my *Francie®* doll and the beginning of my current doll collection, I collected unicorns and Mickey Mouse. My Mickey collection is getting to be pretty huge, but it was becoming less and less fun. After all, how many black mice in red shorts can you have on a shelf? And my unicorn collection, thanks to a stubborn evil black cat that hated everything resembling purity, was turned into a collection of horses with warty foreheads. Then one Christmas, my sister gave me the *Egyptian Queen BARBIE®* doll. I had never seen such a beautiful doll. She was so much nicer than the *BARBIE®* dolls of the late 70s had been. She was like my dolls from the 60s with her fancy clothes and real eyelashes. My life took a dramatic turn for the vinyl right then.

I am a true believer in de-boxing my dolls. I just couldn't stand the thought of seeing them stuck behind a layer of plastic and cardboard, held in bondage by twisty ties, and horror of horror, to have their hair sewn to the box! Even if I'd only take them out one time to check their clothes and touch their hair, I just had to do it. I was starting to feel like a pariah in the world of the Pink Princess. No one understood that they were only valuable to me if I could touch them and play with them.

My creations began about four years ago when I started making *BARBIE®* doll clothes for my niece. I would spend my lunch hours and breaks sewing her tiny clothes by hand while my personal collection kept getting bigger and bigger. I had a swimsuit *BARBIE®* doll with huge eyes that we jokingly called the "ugly naked *BARBIE®* doll" that was used as a mannequin for the clothes I was making and designing.

Then a couple of years later, after seeing the doll makeovers in *Barbie Bazaar* magazine and *Fashion Doll Makeovers*, I decided to give it a try myself. For the next couple of years my mom was the proud recipient of a one-of-a-kind fashion doll makeover for Christmas and her birthday. The first one was pretty over the top, but as time went by, good taste intervened. I learned a lot from Jim's first book: how to reroot, repaint, and make those pretty eyelashes. I would buy fashion magazines and watch all the fashion shows on TV to get good ideas for new and different outfits.

The Ritz

Then during the summer of 1997, I discovered the *Gene®* doll. I could take her out of the box. I could brush her hair. I could change her clothes. I could play with her. It was love. Best of all, I could sew for her on the sewing machine. I wasn't going to go blind hand sewing those tiny little outfits anymore. The *Gene®* doll bug has also bitten my mom, so now she gets outfits for her *Red Venus Gene®* for holidays.

The lack of commercial patterns forced me to learn to do a lot of things I never imagined doing. I couldn't just take a sleeve here and attach it to the bodice there. I had to make things from scratch. I started out with simple stuff that I knew how to make for people and dolls — like the capes and evening gowns. I started doing research about the clothing of the 40s and 50s, and tried to find fashion history books. I'd watch old movies on AMC and TCM to get more ideas. As a child of 'Creature Feature,' it never occurred to me before to watch classy movies! The *Gene®* doll really opened up a whole new world for me.

The most important thing for me when I make an outfit or a doll is for it to be complete. I don't want my customers to be thinking I should have included this or that. I try to include everything I can think of to give my work a finished look that is pleasing to the eye and fun, too. Right now I'm working on trying to make shoes. It's hard, but I'll get it down eventually. I learned how to make jewelry from my best *Gene®* doll friend Teri Wenzel of Lobehangers, and new tricks for hair from my first *Gene®* doll buddy Jay Serle. My sister Reece was the one who showed me not to be afraid to repaint her either. 'Don't worry, if you screw up you can wash it off, and try again.' That was so hard to learn, but I'm telling other people the same thing every day.

I think I've truly become addicted to vinyl. I'm currently collecting the *Gene®* doll, the *Julia®* doll, the Takara *Jenny®* doll and friends, the Magic Attic® dolls, and Robert Tonner's *Tyler Wentworth®* doll. I just love creating for all of them because they have such different personalities. People often ask me why I don't sew for people, and I tell them it's because a person wouldn't be too happy sitting naked on my desk for days or even weeks at a time. They aren't too fond of having pins holding their clothes together or the thought of doing a boiling water perm and they definitely don't come in boxes!"

Dracula's Daughter (jewelry by Lobehangers)

Denis Morf

Creations by Denis Morf

"My name is Denis Morf, born on June 6, 1954 at La Chaux-de-Fonds, in the French speaking part of Switzerland. I am living in Bienne and have worked at a tailor shop for about a year.

Since 1960 I have been passionately dressing the *BARBIE*® doll, not because I like the doll, but because I think she is the model for creating a personality, dress or costume. By the way, I am not working exclusively on the *BARBIE*® doll (I am using the blonde *BARBIE*® doll least). The *Marina*® doll, the *Teresa*® doll, the *Christie*® doll, the *Midge*® doll and others inspire me more. I think they are nearer to reality, especially when looking at their faces. It is always my aim to create a real personality, as credible and natural as possible.

I am mostly influenced by the glamour of Hollywood from the years 1940 to 1960 and am trying to capture that style. Many personalities from Rita Hayworth to Nina Hagen; from Sissy to the singers Siouxsie and the Banshees; the Disney characters Cruella, Cinderella, Mary Poppins, witches; and the stars of the music halls like Josephine Baker, Dalida, Nana Mouskouri, Janis Joplin, Tina Turner, and Marilyn Monroe have come into being as a doll so far.

I am trying to capture the glamour of the costumes of the great eras, too, as well as the ones of various ethnic groups.

One of my great pleasures is to start with the realization of the personality by choosing the appropriate doll and the best material for converting from 1.70m (about 2 yards) to 30cm (12in). Painting the face, styling the hair, posing the doll, making the costumes, beading...what an exciting attempt each time!

In the eighties and nineties I designed and made costumes for the theater and cabaret, and I myself played the cabaret for 15 years. My costumes are well received by the cabaret visitors and the press.

In 1996 I started to exhibit my creations, twice at a fashionable hairdresser's shop in La Neuveville and later, from October 3, 1997 to January 18, 1998, at the Alexis Forel Museum in Morges, Switzerland."

Phedora

DENIS MORF
Rue des Prés 100
2502 Bienne
Suisse

Hello Dolly

Tina

Amy Nardone

Creations by Amy Nardone

"My name is Amy Nardone and I live in Westminster, Maryland. I have a great husband, (Jay) a wonderful son (Jason) and am owned by six cats! As a little girl, I was always playing with BARBIE® dolls up until I turned 13 (my brothers' friends made fun of me and I packed them away). I was also an avid drawer. My mom is a professional artist and I feel I am very lucky to have inherited some of her talent. As I got older, even though the dolls were packed away, I still drew sketches. I would always sketch women in glamorous outfits, using up pads of paper daily drawing new ideas. But that was as far as that talent took me.

I tried many different projects...cross-stitching, calligraphy, theater, anything that I could use my skills for...but nothing satisfied me. After I met Jay, he introduced me to some friends one evening and one woman had a collection of dolls, floor to ceiling of...my favorite childhood doll, the BARBIE® doll. I couldn't believe it! Here was my favorite toy and an adult was collecting her! Well, that started the whole thing.

My first BARBIE® doll was the 2nd Hallmark Christmas doll. From then on I collected everything, not knowing what to buy and what not to buy. Then the Internet came along and I joined a BARBIE® doll group. I met a lot of new people on-line. Next, I started attending doll shows and bought a great book called *Fashion Doll Makeovers* by Jim Faraone. That started the ball rolling. I decided that with all of the sketches I do and all of the ideas I had in my head, I could design my own clothes. I first decided to try my hand at facial painting. My first doll looked like a cross between Tammy Faye Baker and the Bride of Frankenstein. But persistence was paying off. I finally had a use for the talent that I had longed to use for so long. Needless to say, today my dolls look 100% better than my first one. Next, I started rerooting eyelashes and hair. But I had one problem: I had all of these ideas and could not sew to save my life!

I met a woman on the Internet, Janet Rodriguez from Largo, Florida and she and I formed our own business: 'AJ Creations.' I would sketch out exactly what I wanted made and send it with handwritten instructions and material. She would make my design and send it back to me, usually ten at a time. I actually saw my creations come to life. It was amazing! She is such a great seamstress.

I wanted to learn how to sew for myself. I started practicing with patterns and came up with my own to use for my designs. I was given a great sewing machine and serger and put them to good use. So besides the little venture I have with Janet, I also do my own creations, sew everything myself, hand bead, etc. I named the new business 'All Dolled Up.' I am always coming up with new ideas and before anything I do my preliminary sketch. Then I'm off to the sewing room where my creations come to life. It's hard for me to decide which I like better, sewing my designs or repainting the dolls. What a great canvas to use! All of my dolls are facially repainted and eyelashes are rerooted. I also reroot hair and reposition the arms, fingers and hands. What fun! I have sold several designs off the Internet and more than the money, I enjoy hearing about how well my dolls are received. Being in this new book is a dream come true for me! It took me a number of years to find my niche, but now that I have, I couldn't imagine doing anything else!"

ALL DOLLED UP
Amy Nardone
3103 Richwood Ave.
Baltimore, MD 21244
E-mail: anardone@toad.net
Web Site: http://www.toad.net/~anardone

Julie Neises

Creations by Julie Neises

"It seems like it was just yesterday that I was involved in serious *BARBIE*® doll play mode...My doll was quite a gal, cruising on her personal yacht made of Flintstones Building Boulders and traveling with her secret agent companion, Mr. Robot. (Hey, he was a lot more animated than the *Ken*® doll; his head lit up with flashing colored lights and when his batteries ran out, the *BARBIE*® doll had a special compartment for all of her special dolly accessories!) Yes, time flies, children grow up, get married and tend to all those adult responsibilities...well at least most of the time! Years later, during the summer of 1985, the little child inside returned when my sister discovered one of the early *BARBIE*® doll collecting books. It was literally mutilated, with pages falling out from over-perusal. This was also the summer that I announced to my husband, "All I need is that mint *Twiggy*® doll; I really wanted it when I was little...that's the ONLY doll I want." Yeah, right.

Nineteen eighty-nine was the year that I started working as a regular contributor to the *BARBIE*® *Bazaar* magazine, which has been quite an enjoyable activity. With the occasional assistance of my sister Janine, we've done many pictorial articles with a few featuring our own doll artist creations. Some of my creations that I am the most pleased with are those of celebrities. Trying to capture the essence of a particular personality through the meticulous process of hair rerooting, face repainting and fashion designing is a rewarding challenge. All clothing is sewn by hand. (Sewing machines and I just do not mix well; I somehow managed to break my mother's machine years ago by just threading the bobbin!) When I'm not sure how to put together a pair of pants or jacket, I'll take apart an old doll item for research and then make my own pattern.

Creating the Beatles dolls was one of those rewarding challenges. Working on them brought back childhood memories of the days when I longed for a *Ken*® doll that really had hair...Beatle-like hair. (My *Ken*® doll had an odd spotty bald thing going on.) In desperation, the *Ken*® doll often sported one of my *Fashion Queen BARBIE*® doll wigs, but that Beatle illusion just wasn't there...he looked more like Prince Valiant, which was certainly uncool. (Mr. Robot's colorful flashing head was much more attractive!) So this was a creative adventure that satisfied that little child within.

I would say that my favorite *BARBIE*® dolls are those from the Mod period, with the *Francie*® doll topping the list. I enjoyed designing for her when I was little and still do today!

My ambition since childhood — aside from collecting as many dolls as possible — was to be an art teacher. I have earned degrees in fine arts and education, and have taught elementary and secondary art since 1981. Although my first love was painting and drawing, I have worked in bronze sculpture for twenty years and have had pieces exhibited at local competitions and shows.

Despite my background in fine art and education, don't expect me to provide deep analysis of my doll art creations. I think that doll art should be fun. I have fun making it and hope that viewers get similar enjoyment from my work."

JULIE NEISES
P.O. Box 1292
Mishawaka, IN 46546-1292
E-mail: JAFNice@aol.com

Competition piece from 1995 convention

Francie® Rocks makeover

Elvis

The Beatles

Thomas O'Brien

Creations by Thomas O'Brien

"What is it about dolls? I have loved them since the earliest years of my childhood, especially dressable dolls like the *BARBIE*® doll, the *G.I. Joe*® figure, the *Johnny Hero*® doll and the *Tammy*® doll. They bring back some of my fondest memories of being a kid in the sixties. These miniature people with their miniature wardrobes captivated me for hours and hours at a time. Dressing, undressing, and redressing them was something I never tired of. Luckily, my sister had a *BARBIE*® doll and a *Tammy*® doll, since I wasn't allowed to have any of my own. I think I played with them more than she did. Surprisingly, my mother was okay about it. The only stipulation was that I had to put them away before guests came over. So every now and then

I would put them away. Now as an adult I am continuing what I loved as a child, and I can play with my doll collection whenever I want.

My collection runs the gamut from dolls that have been tenderly restored to near mint vintage to new. I couldn't even count the clothing and accessories I have to dress them in. I suppose that explains why I started creating for dolls in the first place. Having so many incomplete outfits and missing certain hard-to-find items, I would attempt to make the missing pieces myself. Some turned out well, others not so well. But I knew from the start that this was something I loved, so I kept at it. My first efforts were simple jewelry and accessory designs. Then I worked up the courage to create my first complete outfit back in 1997. That was the USO Tour '44. Then came the ongoing nursing series, and the snowball goes rolling along. As you can see, I love the tailored little things. They always were and still are the ones that catch my eye.

A love of vintage carries over into my own designs as well. All of my period and uniform designs are researched for accurate detailing. If a certain detail doesn't translate exactly, I will take a bit of creative license. For example, I use zipper and snap closures on most garments, even though the periods of some of my designs pre-date their inventions. Also, beads suffice as buttons for the USO Tour '44, etc. If the illusion is successful, it usually means that the scale and detailing are correct. That's the most important thing. All garments are lined or neatly finished. The tailored suits have lined jackets and most have either a half slip or lining under the skirt.

Experimentation with textures and scales is also a lot of fun. Sometimes you can arrive at the most unexpected combinations. The gown called 'Ice Cream Cake' is flocked dotted organza over white lace over white satin. I liked the sheen of satin and texture of lace showing through the sheer organza. A pink suit entitled 'Beekman Place' has the look of a loopy wool bouclé. It is actually made from a lightweight terry washcloth. I thought the scale and color were just right, and went with it. On a 20's style outfit, 'Tea and Crumpets', the hat is made of felt molded over the rubber cap from a chair leg, then upholstered with the same navy crepe chiffon as the jacket and skirt. The experimentation is one of my favorite parts of the process. That's when the

Blue Moon

creative juices really begin to flow, and great things are bound to happen. I also think that's why so many people have bought my designs.

With a fine arts degree from way back when, I have worked as a graphic designer and illustrator for the past 20 years. Having always worked in two dimensions, the three dimensional aspect of dolls is a welcome change for me. I really wanted to earn my degree in fashion design, but felt insecure about my ability to sew, so I went for a minor in fashion illustration instead, and learned to sew on my own.

After so many years, I haven't lost the desire to design clothes, so I've polished my construction skills, and here I am...and here they are. I hope you have as much fun looking at them as I had creating them. Please send me your questions and comments. I would love to hear from you."

Nurse Series, (left to right) '40's Nurse, '10's Nurse, 19th Century Nurse

Donald W. Philpott

Creations by Don W. Philpott

"I started out as a gymnast when I was five years old. I always loved to dance and started taking ballet classes when I was a teenager. I got a scholarship to the Dance Theater of Harlem in 1974 and performed with them until 1976. I then moved on to dance with different companies in New York, New Jersey, and Boston. I later decided that, though ballet would always be my first love, I decided I would move towards theater dance.

I studied jazz and tap and took singing lessons and then decided to get a degree in dance, so I went to Julliard School of the Arts.

I performed in 'West Side Story,' 'Pippin,' 'Guys and Dolls' and other shows on tour and in summer stock theater. I've also been in music videos and a couple of movie musicals. In addition, I have begun to choreograph more, which I love to do because I love to create.

I enjoy collecting things. I collect everything from fashion dolls to records. I also like to sculpt both in clay and soft sculpture.

Earlier I was into collecting *BARBIE*® dolls and I still love her. About six or seven years ago a friend told me that Mel Odom was working on his own doll and would be coming out with her soon. I was familiar with Mel's work as an illustrator and so I knew that his doll would be beautiful. When the *Gene*® doll came out I went crazy collecting her, just like everyone else. I spoke to Mel at the first *Gene*® Doll Convention and then later the next year at a friend's *Gene*® doll party. During our conversation he expressed the desire to create an African-American friend for the *Gene*® doll but he didn't know when or if Ashton Drake® would do one.

I got inspired by the conversation and decided to try making one of my own. I got the idea from an article in *Barbie Bazaar*® magazine, which discussed how to dye the *BARBIE*® doll and the *Francie*® doll. I tried the process on the *Gene*® doll, but it turned out to be a little more complicated and I had to make adjustments. I finally came up with a *Gene*® doll that really looked good and she became Josephine Baker, which was my first entry into the *Gene*® doll contest at the Halloween convention. I didn't win anything but she went over really well.

Everyone started talking about a bent-leg *Gene*® doll and how it could be really nice. Now, one thing I had always hated about doll companies that produce fashion dolls is that they would make ballet outfits and point shoes for a doll whose feet are designed for high-heeled shoes. I always thought that they looked silly in the shoes because they were never really on point.

I decided to try a little surgery and came up with two dolls, 'Sheherazade' and 'The Firebird.' I entered both of them into a one-of-a-kind auction at the 1998 *Gene*® Doll Convention and was proud that they were received so well. 'Sheherazade' actually broke a record as the first non-Ashton Drake® design to go as high as it did. I'm just glad it did its' part in raising money to fight AIDS.

I plan to do a line of dancers both ethnic and Caucasian. I also want to work with dolls like the *Cissy*® doll and other fashion dolls.

My ultimate goal is to make my own doll. I already have the design. There's just the minor problem of money. Oh well...."

Inspired by a Brazilian friend with light brown skin with a slightly red tint.

The Dancer

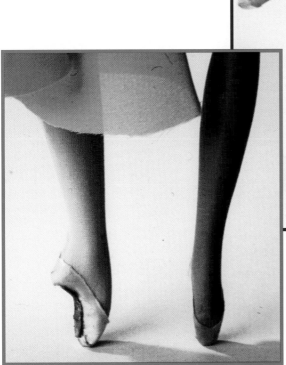

DON W. PHILPOTT
484 W. 43rd St., #21H
New York, N.Y. 10036
E-mail: Billiwin4k@aol.com

Steven Pim/Grant Salminen/ Jennifer Scaff King

Creations by Steven Pim/
Grant Salminen/
Jennifer Scaff King
Photos by Wayne Fettig

"The San Francisco Doll Artists are Grant Salminen, Jennifer Scaff King and Steven Pim. We have been creating doll art for store windows and art galleries in the bay area since 1996. We love using fashion dolls to portray characters and scenes from contemporary urban life, political issues and pop culture. We know we've been successful when people do a double take, laugh and bring their friends back to see our work.

Our dolls have been featured in several bay area publications. The exhibit at San Francisco Airport was installed in November of 1996, and due to its popularity, ran for six months. The dolls can be seen in many bay area locations."

"I'm Steven Pim and I collected *BARBIE*® dolls as a child back in Ohio in the 60s. Doll art began for me with a Christmas store window in the late 1980s. By the 1990s, the tableaux became quite elaborate. In an attempt to reflect the diversity of life in the world and especially San Francisco, I began creating dolls with facial hair, jewelry and unique clothing.

Having a degree in theater, I treat the window like a stage. Once the 'script' is written, I design the sets and props and costume the cast. Dolls are such cooperative actors!

I joined the San Francisco *BARBIE*® Doll Club (now the SF Fashion Doll Club) and met Grant Salminen, a doll restorer artist. After helping me clean and restore a large collection, he expressed interest in helping with my store windows. He's taken the art of doll miniatures to a new height!"

"I'm Grant Salminen and in 1984, I began doing *BARBIE*® doll restoration as a career. With a background in electronics and mechanical design, I was a printed circuit board designer, so it was easy for me to adapt to the 1/6-scale world of fashion dolls. I had been collecting for about 15 years when I joined the SF Club and met Steven Pim.

Using various art materials and fine paintbrushes to redo dolls' faces and furniture, I was able to help create even more realistic and detailed installations. By traveling the doll show circuit, we are happy to share our art beyond the immediate bay area."

"I'm Jennifer Scaff King and I hated dolls as a child, so I was very surprised when the inspiration came to me to create the Venus of Willendorf. I recreated the goddess icon of ancient times, using the icon of our times that I previously loved to hate. Much to my horror, I began to collect cast-off dolls from young friends and relatives, making them into different goddess images.

The inspiration came from a combination of my mother's anthropological studies of ancient goddess cultures and the amazing store windows of Steven Pim, which were for many years the highlights of the North Polk Street neighborhood in San Francisco.

I finally got up the courage to introduce myself to Steven and show him some of my work. I was thrilled when he liked it and used it in the San Francisco Airport exhibit. We went on to collaborate with Grant on windows at Ozzie's Soda Fountain in the Elmwood Pharmacy in Berkeley, and look forward to doing displays for some 40th birthday events as the San Francisco Doll Artists."

Biker Boys by Grant Salminen

Doll by Grant Salminen

Dolls by Steven Pim

Divine by Grant Salminen

Nefertiti, Goddess of
Willendorf and Death of Venus
by Jennifer Scaff King

Vickie Peterson Rubie

Creations by
Vickie Peterson Rubie

"I have loved to sew for as long as I can remember. I think I got my first doll at age six, a black-haired #5, and sewing and the *BARBIE®* doll have always gone together for me. My mom and her friends saved scraps for me and I started sewing doll clothes for myself as well as my mom's friends' kids and grandkids, to earn extra money at Christmas time. I didn't really use patterns; I just cut the pieces out of the fabrics and fit them together.

I hid my *BARBIE®* dolls and her friends in the bottom of my college trunk, being afraid they'd end up in some rummage sale while I was away. They were always there when I needed friends. I was an art major with an emphasis in metal-smithing. I fabricated a miniature brass bed, *BARBIE®* doll-sized, for a project. My instructor mentioned that it looked perfect for the *BARBIE®* doll and I was too embarrassed to tell him that, indeed, was

what I had in mind. I'm very happy those secretive, closet-collecting days are over! I collect mostly vintage, but also some of the new dolls.

Lately I've been making kimonos for the *BARBIE®* doll and her friends and the *Gene®* doll to sell on eBay. I've had a wonderful time corresponding with people all over the world, and at the same time, helping to support my *BARBIE®* doll habits.

I have been interested in Japanese culture and costuming for a long time. In college I started making art-quilt kimonos, wearable, but heavily quilted and adorned with 3-D fabric sculptures, sometimes inside out. I love the simplicity of the kimono style, the straight strips of fabric that can be worked and then sewn together.

With my three children, ages 16, 12 and 8, demanding more time and me wanting to give it, quilting the large pieces has become harder and harder. By making smaller pieces that can be done in stages and stored in a tray, I'm fulfilling a creative need sewing kimonos for the *BARBIE®* doll and the *Gene®* doll. I make small productions of each color, and I can sit down for a short time or a whole day and work on the stages. I have also become very good at organizing the pieces that need close handwork so I can take them to the baseball game, on a road trip, or complete them while watching a movie. Sometimes my family even grabs a handful to help out!

I have never lived in Japan, but have looked at lots of books and was greatly inspired by the *BARBIE® in Japan book*. I have heard from a few Japanese people correcting the styles I do or giving suggestions, and sometimes even offering resource information. I am very happy to get these suggestions, but I also think part of the fun is that my styles are quite spontaneous, and since I don't know much about the traditions, I am not inhibited to put certain colors or fabrics together. I designed my own kimono pattern and search for fabric wherever I go.

My matador costumes were originally done for competition at the Albuquerque convention. I did research the traditions of the Matador; the salmon pink socks, the incredibly tight trousers, and the hat with a braid of hair attached. I had a wonderful time finding trims and fabrics that would give the right look in the right scale. I usually sell the dolls dressed because the fit is so snug and close that I'm afraid of too many try-ons with the semi-fragile fabrics.

Spanish Dancer and Matador

I have lived in Montana almost all my life. If we are lucky our area has a couple of doll shows a year. I've been lucky enough to go to two national *BARBIE®* conventions in San Diego and Albuquerque, where I participated in the competitions.

Inspiration comes from everywhere. It's so fun to be openly creating and trading and doing something that brings me so much joy, both in the fabrication and knowing others are pleased by my works. My family still has somewhat of a hard time with all of this, but I'm hoping that with time they will understand. I have a local group of friends that get together once a month or so to share our finds. The Internet has also opened up a whole new world of friendship.

When I'm not doing the doll designing, I also love doing stained glass, quilting, snow skiing, sewing for my kids, tennis, and of course spending time with my family. We are about to begin building a new home that will include a wonderful doll display/sewing room, where I know I'll be in heaven!"

Crane kimonos for the *Gene®* doll

Nautical Skooter

Imelda Sanchez

Creations by Imelda Sanchez

"It all started three and a half years ago in a local bookstore. My boyfriend was becoming frustrated (or was it scared?) over my obsession with tattoo magazines. I had no intentions of ever getting a tattoo; it was the magnificent artwork that mesmerized me. I had always wanted to be an artist when I was growing up and spent countless hours drawing figures. Upon graduating from high school in 1977, I pursued a degree in advertising art. I quickly realized that this was not what I had in mind for my artistic outlet, so I left school and entered the 'normal' working class. That continued until my boyfriend replaced the tattoo magazines in my hand with a doll magazine. Everything changed for me from that day forward. I rediscovered my favorite childhood doll, the *BARBIE*® doll, and realized for the first time that she was not just a toy for children anymore.

It wasn't long after that day that I designed my first doll. She was a showgirl that I repainted using markers and model paints. Needless to say, she did not turn out very well and I was ready to give up when my friend Dorothy Fannin came to my rescue with detailed instructions she obtained from the Internet. It's amazing what the correct materials and tools will accomplish! I started creating then and although I still have my 'normal' job, I have discovered a wonderful hobby that brings me a great deal of pleasure.

I have been asked many times why I call myself Mariza's Custom Dolls instead of using my own name. The name Mariza symbolizes femininity, sensuality and self-assurance and the dolls I create are one or a combination of all those things. From sexy lingerie to exotic harem dancers, I live many of my fantasies through my dolls. They also provide me with the artistic outlet I've desired for years."

Charise

Betty Page

Lady in Red

Ivana

George Sarofeen

Creations by George Sarofeen

"Born in Quincy, Massachusetts and raised in Colonial Heights, Virginia, I was the youngest of four baby boomers. Much to the concern of my father and the support of my mother, I was fascinated with costumes and clothing for as long as I can recall. I think it all started when, with a pale blue crayon, I colored Cinderella's ball gown in a Disney coloring book in the early 1960s. Her gown was the most beautiful thing I had ever seen. I stared at her for hours wondering how I could make one of those dresses for myself! Years later when the high school drama club needed costumes for a production of 'The Lottery,' I raided my mother's clothes in the basement and pulled together the women's costumes. The garments weren't exactly Cinderella's ball gown, but those girls made some pretty convincing farmer's wives! This aesthetic success was followed by buying patterns and fabrics for our drama club production of 'Dracula' and directing an army of mothers to create the costumes. My career had started!

I eventually landed in college only to find that pre-med. studies and I did not mix. I changed my major and earned a BA in theater arts at Virginia Tech. Thinking I was destined to be a star of stage and screen, during my college years I somehow found myself drawn to the costume shop. Here, I found that my heart was not on the stage but in supporting those who were by creating costumes for their characters. I was not the best tailor at the time, so in an effort to enhance my sewing skills, I entered an all female fortress and became the first male to enroll in the School of Clothing, Textiles and Related Arts.

This groundbreaking experience for the male gender at the age of 21 helped to propel me to graduate school studying for a Masters of Fine Arts in costume design at Temple University. It was there that I found my true appreciation for the theatrical, concentrating my efforts on learning the art of millinery and period patterning.

Since that time, I have been designing costumes professionally for 23 years. Twenty-one years of that time I was the senior costume designer at Paramount Parks, the theme park extension of Paramount Pictures. As a result of this wonderful experience, I designed over 6000 costumes for musical reviews, television shows, ice spectacles, Las Vegas shows and industrial shows. Currently, my designs can be seen at Star Trek: The Experience and on cruise ships within the Renaissance Cruise Line and Royal Caribbean Cruise Line fleets.

Because I had the fortune to create very theatrical clothing for real women for these many years, I did not engage my talents in creating

Gala Event

garments for dolls until recently. I began to (allowed myself to) collect fashion dolls after I turned 40. I was always fascinated with the history of costume and as an extension of this fascination I began to attend doll shows and doll conventions and read doll magazines. A whole world with which I was unfamiliar was revealed to me. As I saw all the fascinating creations that the many talented doll artists displayed, I experienced an epiphany! Suddenly, it dawned on me that I could do this. Designing for dolls would use the skills that I had acquired over the years - and the models wouldn't squeal if you accidentally stuck them with a pin.

I love to create 'glamour' garments, which involve stitching beads and sequins. An avid needlepoint artist, I have found the involvement of using my hands to create and embellish garments is my favorite part of designing for fashion dolls. Sometimes I will spend over 80 hours working on a doll such as 'The Belle of New York,' which was created for a one-of-a-kind auction at the 1998 *Gene®* Doll Convention. She is embellished with over 2000 'seed pearls' on ecru lace and raised $2,600 at the auction.

Often I will buy fabric and study it for days and weeks before I create a garment. I use fabrics that are properly scaled for the doll I am creating not only in pattern, but also in draping weight. Once I make a decision about what to do with the fabric, I begin to work, but always remain flexible to change as the process advances. I purchase only enough fabric to create a garment once, for I love working in the moment producing original one-of-a-kind dolls.

When asked what my favorite part of creating designs for dolls is, I always respond that I love to create dolls for auctions. It's a great way to contribute to the benefit of people who are in need. Doll artists who share their talent in this way are very lucky. Knowing that one doll can raise thousands of dollars for a charitable organization and that doll was made with one's own hands warms the heart like no other experience I have ever known."

GEORGE SAROFEEN
141 LaFayette Circle
Cincinnati, OH 45220
BarbiDude@aol.com

Walking
Mermaid

The Belle of
New York

Jenn Scully

Creations by Jenn Scully

"I started collecting dolls at a very young age, almost from birth actually. My grandmother, Helen, got me started. I was born in December and for every Christmas I can remember as a child she gave me a doll. Not just any doll, but ones that someday would be worth something more than just fond memories. As I grew up, I remember taking the train into Chicago with my mother and grandmother and going window shopping around the holidays. I remember being so small and the city being so big and taking escalators up to the toy floor in Carson Pieri Scotts. There was every toy imaginable there, like FAO Schwartz today, but decorated for Christmas. Here my grandmother would let me pick out dolls I liked. Well, not necessarily let me, she had no choice because I would often grab them off the shelf and show her. I had no idea that the dolls I showed her would end up under the Christmas tree.

The last ten years or so, I hadn't even thought about that doll collection. I was going through my school years and had other things to concentrate on. Now that I am married, I have been overcome with a need to save things, or memories. Basically, I wanted to start collecting something again. I already had a collection sitting under my nose, so I decided to continue that. And boy have I.

So, that's how I got started collecting dolls. I still have every one of those dolls I got for Christmas when I was young. My grandmother visited my mother and I in my previous home in Virginia not too long ago, and the three of us dragged out the four very large moving boxes that hold my 26-year-old doll collection. We took out each and every one of those dolls, looking at them all in their turn. There were three generations of us all admiring a collection of simple dolls, each of us sitting in relative silence, our minds recalling our own personal memories we had with those dolls.

I started collecting again about three years ago, and I already have around 150 new *BARBIE*® dolls and am addicted to Franklin Mint® dolls (Thanks, Grammy). In the past two years, I have started customizing *BARBIE*® dolls. This was a major undertaking for me, since I had only sewn quilts and curtains prior to the *BARBIE*® dolls. My mother's favorite thing to mention when talking about my dolls and me is, 'It took her six weeks to sew a sweatshirt in junior high school!' And she was right. I was never good at sewing clothes.

I basically have no training in the sewing arts. I was involved in theater quite a bit in college as a costume designer, lighting and set designer, but I never sewed. I always used found items for my costume designs. I can't draw very well, so I don't sketch my designs before I sew them. Basically, I work from the seat of my pants and from a vision I have in my head generated by the fabrics and trims I find. All I know is that I now enjoy spending a whole day in my sewing room, making things of beauty from my own two uncoordinated hands.

I have no idea what made me sit down at my sewing machine one day and sew a *BARBIE*® doll dress, but I did, and haven't stopped since. I have made over 40 dolls, not to mention the ones that didn't turn out to my liking, and not one of them have been the same. I find great happiness in shopping for fabric, cutting something out, hoping it will fit, then maybe turning it into something great. I think it is the adventure of the unknown that makes it fun.

I consider myself very lucky to have a husband and family who support me in my hobby and two wonderful puppies that thankfully leave my *BARBIE*® dolls and fabric alone. The four of us live very happily up on top of a mountain in the Colorado

JENN SCULLY
9215 Sandy Lane
Conifer, CO 80433
E-mail: jbp@employees.org
Web Site: http://www.employees.org:80/~jbp/index.html

Rockies, just having moved here in August of 1998 from Virginia. I have a BA in history from George Mason University in Fairfax Virginia, and I used to own a cake decorating company. I am still a quilter, and sew quilts for a local non-profit organization named 'People Comforters.' We mainly sew quilts for police and firemen to carry around in their cars to give to people who suffer from severe traumas. We also make booties and toiletry bags for a local single mother's home and battered women's shelters. I am also currently secretary of the local *BAR-BIE*® doll club, The Fashion Doll Club of the Rockies. Thanks to everyone who has given me the encouragement to pursue my sewing in all forms, and to all the people who have bought and enjoy my dolls to this very day."

Debbie Silva

Creations by Debbie Silva

"Not long ago, I was guilty of saying 'Dolls? Dolls?? Who in their right mind collects dolls?' Today I have 14 *Gene*® dolls, and my collection is growing.

About a year ago, my friend and hair stylist Reba told me she was designing a doll to enter in a competition at a doll convention. She thought I should make one as well. 'Right, I thought. I really have time to mess with dolls.' Reba was persistent, and introduced me to the *Gene*® doll in 'Monaco' and several other outfits. Something about the *Gene*® doll caught my interest. Reba lent 'Monaco' to me, and I began my first gown.

I quickly found my inspiration in a mossy green distressed satin fabric. I could just see it covered with pink ribbon and rose vines. The marathon began. I embroidered and beaded that dress in hotel rooms, airports and at home for the next eight weeks. I finished the dress hours before the start of the 1998 West Coast *Gene*® Doll Convention. By that time, I could hardly stand the sight of the dress, and my fingers felt like pincushions.

Fate didn't seem to be on my side the day I left for the convention. I arrived at the airport with a borrowed *Midnight Romance Gene*® doll dressed in my creation only to find that the plane had been delayed by four hours. Some idiot made a joke about a bomb scare, and the entire plane was delayed. But I finally arrived at the Roosevelt Hotel with doll in hand, and I had a blast. The convention was fun, and the people were outstanding. I was truly hooked. Of course, it didn't hurt that "And The Winner Is...." won first place in the amateur gala events category!

After the convention, Reba introduced me to other *Gene*® doll collectors (Kristan, Chris, Kim and Reba) in the San Jose area. We became known as the San Jose Forumites, and meet at least once a month to share our loot. Thanks, Reba!

Kathryn

Christine Daae — repaint by Ken Bartram

I have always loved costuming. Over the years, I've made Elizabethan costumes to wear to the Renaissance Fair and Victorian dresses just for fun. Doll costuming is a perfect outlet for my passion for historical dress and for fancy embroidery. And best of all, the *Gene*® doll doesn't change size from fitting to fitting, although working on such a small scale does have its moments."

DEBBIE SILVA
781 Teresi Court
San Jose, CA 95117
E-mail:dsilva@bridgeware.com
or
desilva@worldnet.att.net

Hannibal Dancer — repaint by Ken Bartram

First place winner at the 1998 West Coast convention — repaint by Mary Beyer.

Helen R. Skinner

Creations by Helen R. Skinner

"One of my very oldest memories is that of sitting on the old farmhouse front porch, playing with a bobby pin doll. She was a lovely ballerina consisting of three bobby pins (one for the body and two long pointed twirling legs) and one of my dad's beautiful flowers confiscated for a tutu. With five older sisters I learned quickly how to improvise, for toys and dolls were high on the list. Through the years I remember hours of endless fun, dressing the real dolls that I had. The *BARBIE*® doll was at the top of my favorites list, and her 'Solo' dress had not a sparkly left after so much use.

Fashion dolls grew from childhood companions to an adult interest for me. Historical costumes and fashions that reflect those times became a focus on porcelain dolls I have had for years.

Michael and I have five wonderful children. They all know Mom is obsessed with dolls. After years of having doll parts and cloth all around, they just assume they are a normal part of the furniture. Considering their lack of interest in my hobby, they have really been very supportive and understanding! Doll show assistants and fashion commentary are always available in our home. My wonderful Aunt Rose is even involved now. Her snoods for the *Gene*® doll fashions are complimenting many of my designs.

The last two years I have spent designing and repainting the *Gene*® doll. With such versatility and beauty, she is the perfect lady to create for. From her head to her toes, I try to make everything. Shoes seem to be a big challenge that I enjoy. I hope to keep improving my techniques as I go, and I find that using real leather gives me the look I want. I use Super Sculpy to make the soles and bake up a big batch in the oven. The great variety in colors and the ease in shaping it make it my favorite medium. Sculpy III bakes up nice and firm, ready to attach all kinds of materials to form those matching accessories.

Painting new faces on the dolls brings them to life for me. Each one has its own quality and using acrylics on vinyl is even better than the long, drawn out process I am used to with china painting. A good layer of clear matt sealer is easier than firing the paint, too!

One tip I love to share with other crafters is the glue I use. When doing purses, shoes and hats, BOND® grip glue is perfect since it's tacky right away and holds so well, especially on shoe tops.

As more and more doll enthusiasts share the love of fashion and doll art, I find new friends along the way. That is truly one of the best rewards of a hobby which has enriched our whole family's lives."

Nita Stacy

Creations by Nita Stacy

"Sometimes things just seem to be — as if it's destiny, or fate, or the result of the natural order of chaos. Dollusions by Nita Stacy is one of those things, the creative conclusion of many years of experience, skill and some very happy accidents. In my doll design work, I combine all my artistic talents with professional graphic design to create breath-taking, heart pounding, pulse quickening, gut wrenching or even heart breaking fashion doll art.

I grew up drawing, painting and sewing from an early age, focusing on painting portraits by the time I was in high school. In college I got a degree in advertising/design with a concentration on illustrating/painting and a little sculpture thrown in for good measure. As a professional graphic designer, I've written and illustrated books, designed posters for such events as the 96 Olympics and created packaging for several beverage companies. For a while I was doing nothing but beer label design and referred to myself as the 'Beverage Queen.' Then after working 15 plus years in advertising; creating award winning

Claire

DOLLUSIONS
Nita Stacy
1550 Terrell Mill Rd., #18A
Marietta, GA 30067
Web Site: www.nitastacy.com
or by connecting through
Blumington's Department Store
www.blumingtons.com

Christmas in the City

75

designs for clients such as Coors and Coca Cola, I yearned to do what I did best, more figural-type work: portrait painting plus I had a knack for creating in three dimension. I was very familiar with all the doll art on the market and knew I had something to create.

In a short time, my dolls have become some of the most cherished and sought after by collectors. I believe it's because I'm combining my graphic design experience with fine art training, a quirky sense of the appealing and/or appalling and an interest in dolls. In doing so, I'm able to create at the highest level. One of the reasons doll design is so personally rewarding for me is that I get immediate feedback on how much each owner of one of my dolls loves her. Another thing that sets my dolls apart is that I strive for the unexpected. I like to use subject matter you wouldn't necessarily think you'd find in a fashion doll. I love melancholy, sad stuff - which has led me to create my own versions of Ophelia, Hester Prynne from the Scarlet Letter and even a ghost from the old movie, 'The Uninvited.'

Influenced by my graphic design experience, each of my dollusions has a name and logo designed for her, plus a story. I roam antique shops and flea markets looking for little things like antique jewelry or lace that often become the inspiration for my designs. Other inspiration for my dolls comes from vintage illustrations and photos found in old advertising, postcards, magazines, books and of course old movies. Each of my dolls begins with a sketch, research, and a few more sketches - then I pull together all the materials needed. Using the finest of fabrics and trim, I try to make the clothing as real as possible - just like normal-sized clothes, but small. Deciding what to do is easy, I just think "Hmmm...what would I like in a doll?...What would I like to have in my collection?' Of course, then it's so hard to let her go because it was something I wanted myself.

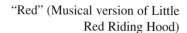

"Rose" (Titanic)

"Red" (Musical version of Little Red Riding Hood)

Great attention to every detail can cause each doll to take as long as a week to complete. Most of my dolls come with little accessories that round out the story of who they are. One of the biggest reasons people love my dollusions is the hand painted faces. I use my skills as a portrait artist here - and that is how I perceive these face paintings. I paint them just like I would a portrait, except I'm working in 3D on vinyl. People often say to me, 'As soon as I saw the face on that doll, I knew it was yours.'

When I first began this venture, my friends and family, not to mention my professional peers, thought I was crazy. I'd get E-mail from former coworkers saying they'd happened upon my web page and couldn't believe what I was doing, although some said they should have suspected because of the vintage *BARBIE*® doll calendar that graced my office wall. Crazy? 'Yes,' I say, 'I am.... I'm dollusional!'"

Arabella Stewart

Creations by Arabella Stewart

"Although on occasion I create a contemporary ensemble, my chosen specialty is designing doll costumes to replicate the various fashions popular throughout history. For me, designing fashion dolls in historical costumes represents the culmination of my love and extensive knowledge of history, a talent for designing, and a childhood passion for playing with my dolls, dollhouse and paper dolls. Yet, despite studying art and fashion design in Manhattan during the 1960s, it wasn't until some 30 years later that the opportunity presented itself for me to indulge myself and start Arabella Stewart Designs.

For the past 10 years, I have lived in an area of rural Maryland where the demand for historically dressed dolls is nearly non-existent and so, when I initially established my fashion house for dolls, I concentrated instead on making both replica and original bridal gowns for 11½-inch dolls. Then I was introduced to cyberspace. I soon discovered that with the entire world at my fingertips I was no longer limited to making only the type of doll that was marketable locally, but instead was now free to devote myself to my first love, the re-creation of historical characters. Subsequently, in 1996 Robert Michael of Global Marketing Services took me under his very capable wing and while I devoted myself to designing and making many of my First Edition historical dolls, he designed my web site and brought my dolls to the attention of a world-wide audience of collectors.

I have often been asked how one of my historically dressed dolls and its design was conceived or developed. Following a lifetime of research history, most of the prominent characters who have used the world as their stage have come alive for me and most often it is one of these ageless monuments upon the pages of history who is my initial inspiration. Further inspiration may come from the color or texture of a rich fabric or a unique trim or perhaps from a special event in the character's life.

Although infrequent, on occasion it has been the discovery of a particular doll that initially inspired me to recreate the character rather than the other way around. My version of an elderly Queen Victoria could not have been possible if I hadn't discovered such a perfect doll to represent her.

Although I have a preference for working with 11½-inch fashion dolls, I have been given the opportunity to create some really beautiful historically dressed *Gene*® dolls, including a Medieval Duchess and several versions of Marie Antoinette, among others. Selecting which doll I will use for a new design depends upon the character I am portraying. While Mattel's *BARBIE*® doll, *Ken*® doll and their extended friends and family work well for some of my designs, in the past year I have been introduced to the *Candi*® dolls, which are available in a wonderful selection of face molds and colorings that I find to be a

Elizabeth I

Louis XVI of France

Macbeth

highly realistic representation of the characters I portray. I find that I am using them more and more frequently. Along the way I have also discovered some 12-inch male action dolls that have worked extremely well for me in my re-creations.

I particularly love fine fabrics, and if they are of heirloom quality or vintage in age I love them even more. I frequently travel overseas and never pass up an opportunity to search out fabrics, trims, or any item that can be used to enhance the individuality of my dolls. I am also indebted to my sister, Sue Coady, who is always searching for exquisite fabrics for me in many of the exotic locations she visits.

Once I have chosen the doll and the historic character or time period I wish to portray, I design and sketch the costume, keeping in mind the fabric and colors I have previously selected. I then make the pattern based upon my sketch. After cutting the pattern, it's time for repaints when necessary or desirable, and hair styling, which in itself can be a time-consuming project since many of the historical hair fashions can be quite complicated. Appropriate undergarments and hose are then made and fitted on the doll. Next in the creative process comes the costume itself. Most of my designs demand layers and I continue working on each piece until the ensemble is complete. As my dolls go to new homes fully attired, many with hand-crafted accessories, it is at this stage that I make whatever additional accessories are going to be included. Once I am satisfied with the final product, I then sign the doll's hang tag, guaranteeing the client that I have personally hand-crafted the doll.

I do, of course, accept commissions to recreate some (but not all!) of my First Editions. I would like to point out that it is of prime importance to me that each and every collector who owns an Arabella Stewart doll is assured that they possess the only doll like it in the world. I always take great care when commissioned to remake a doll to alter the costume just enough to ensure its uniqueness.

A few months ago, I was contacted by one of the shopping channel representatives who was interested in offering my dolls for sale through the show. I was very flattered by their interest, but after careful consideration I decided that I prefer to keep my dolls available only on an exclusive basis rather than mass-produced and marketed.

Not including the vast amounts of time I devote to researching each individual character or historical era, I have found that it takes me approximately 40 hours of exacting labor to complete each doll, and yet, I can honestly say that every moment of it is, to me, a genuine labor of love."

Barbara Stewart

"I bought my first *BARBIE*® doll for my daughter in the 1960s. I remember one Christmas I made 33 outfits for this doll and got a great deal of pleasure watching Nan open all the packages. As it turned out, I think I enjoyed the doll much more than Nan did. Her interest in the *BARBIE*® doll did not last all that long and we put them in the attic.

Years later, Nan produced two granddaughters for me, and my son Andy gave me one granddaughter. Now this was my real chance, and I took advantage of it. All three of those wonderful little girls love the *BARBIE*® dolls, and I began sewing again. I even still had some of the patterns left from the 1960's. After a while, these little girls had the best-dressed *BARBIE*® dolls in town, and all their friends wanted to come to their house to play. Still, I wasn't through creating for this wonderful doll. I decided on a whim to see if I could sell some of my designs, and found that a great number of people were interested in them.

I have done doll shows from Maine to Florida as well as inland. I have sold a lot of dolls and made wonderful friends. I love seeing my repeat customers when I go to shows.

One of the best shows I ever did was in Greensburg, Pennsylvania. I did well at the show, but the best thing that happened to me there was meeting Nancy Parsons. Nancy was the chairperson for the 1999 *BARBIE*® Doll

Creations by Barbara Stewart
Photos by Wesley Stewart

Sunflowers Galore - Sweater, hat and purse knitted

Victorian Era - *Teresa*® doll

Gibson Girl - *Candi*® doll

Convention held in Pittsburgh, Pennsylvania. To make a long story short, Nancy commissioned me to design the convention doll. I had a wonderful time working with her and certainly enjoyed doing the doll.

I have lived in the Carolinas most of my life. I graduated from Hickory High School in Hickory, North Carolina. I took piano lessons most of my young life, and when I went to college at Appalachian State University in Boone, North Carolina, I majored in music. I graduated magna cum laude and have been teaching piano privately for over thirty years. For the past several years, my obsession with the *BARBIE*® doll has caused me to take fewer and fewer students and devote more time to my dolls. As a result, I have kept the cream of the crop in piano students and still have time to create for the *BARBIE*® doll. Life is good!

I try to limit my dolls to no more than ten, but many of them are one-of-a-kind as well. Sometimes I put so much time into one that I don't really want to duplicate it. When I was in college I minored in history, so I am especially interested in duplicating historical outfits. I have tons of patterns and sometimes use them as they are, but most often I redo them to suit myself. I love shopping for fabrics and trims, and know most of the fabric shops on the East Coast! I even managed to wedge myself into the wholesale market for the 1999 convention doll, but that will probably be a one shot deal. I usually don't buy enough of any one fabric to merit buying wholesale.

I like to repaint the dolls' faces. It is fun to see if I can make them look like a particular person. I don't reroot their hair, but I do re-wig them. In fact, most of my dolls have new wigs permanently attached. I also like to root eyelashes for them, like Chuck Kamper taught me. This is one of the wonderful friendships I have made on the doll circuit. Chuck and I share our secrets with each other even though we are in competition.

One of the things I do for the *BARBIE*® doll is design sweaters. Quite often I start with a piece of fabric and let that dictate the design I put on the sweater. I ran into a man from Heartfelt Collectibles in Raleigh, North Carolina last year and he commissioned me to design sweaters for his teddy bears. I spent a great deal of time during the summer of 1998 doing just that. All of the sweaters I do for the *BARBIE*® dolls are hand-knitted as well."

Old World Santa - *Ken*® doll

Mark Twain - *Ken*® doll

LU-BAR DESIGNS
Barbara Stewart
438 Armfield St.
Statesville, NC 28677

David White

Creations by David White

"My interest in design was developed at the university where I studied fine art, interiors and fashion. Which direction to pursue was the hardest decision I had to make. Working in miniature allowed me to encompass different design concepts and concluded in my graduation show held in the Mall Gallery London in the summer of 1996.

Since then I have been working as a freelance designer. My passion is design and I have developed work for cards, books, dolls and interiors.

I have been working in this style for such a short period that I'm still in the learning process. The great success I have found since my first year has encouraged me to continue and succeed.

One positive aspect of this type of work is the ability to use the finest materials, including cashmere, silk, velvet and crystal beads, due to the very small scale. Weight and thickness can still be a problem, but with determination and patience this can be overcome. Scale is always something to consider. Since I prefer to use simple, plain fabrics I have the opportunity to add decoration.

In some cases I buy materials not knowing how I'll use them, but add them to an extensive range of items, just in case. Than I am able to create pieces using this varied palette. For example, I have found that very small

miniature doll picture frames make great belt buckles. In many situations it is this resourcefulness that makes the piece rather than how much money you spend on it.

It's times like these that make copies very profitable, when you can piece together both items. I prefer to make each new piece different by creating each one individually but with the same philosophy in mind. Less is more. Whether it is a day-wear piece or eveningwear, I try not to over-complicate. By using the correct proportions of fabric and color sometimes all that is needed is a simple pair of earrings.

I have so many inspirations and interests that I hardly have enough time to create all these original pieces, let alone copy them. All the luxurious fabrics and great dolls provide enough of a dilemma.

When I research a new collection, I might have only a rough idea, and by the time I've collected hundreds of samples and dolls the outcome could be quite different. This is where I have the biggest problem; due to the time involved my work is quite expensive. I try to set aside one week for each piece.

I try to use a variety of dolls from all different price ranges. It's not always easy to find the right look and the expensive dolls are not always the best. It is undoubtedly satisfying when an ordinary doll turns into an exceptional piece of work. It is this quality that gives me the most inspiration. I'm often surprised how adaptable the *BARBIE*® doll can be. Just the variety of hair colors can dramatically alter the appearance of a look, not to mention skin tones and makeup. The possibilities are really endless."

DAVID WHITE
The Studio
23 The Downlands
Warminster, Wiltshire
BA12 OBD, England

Denise White

Creations by Denise White

"The *BARBIE*® doll and I go back a long way. As a child, my mother thought she was an appropriate doll for a young girl. I thought she was boring, and put her clothes on my Breyer horses. About nine years ago I discovered her with love. I was in a Toys R Us and saw these beautiful dolls...but I was afraid of what friends and family would say if I brought one home. Then I married and moved from Michigan to Illinois and became very ill. I got my first *BARBIE*® doll and she brightened my world. I would save my quarters and buy a doll when I could. When I was sick and couldn't get out of bed I'd look at the dolls.... they were magical and I loved them.

Then about six years ago I went to a doll show. It was heaven! I never knew there were so many *BARBIE*® dolls. I saw the work of a doll artist that was fantastic, so I thought I'd try to do the same. About four years later, here I am...a doll artist. I never dreamed I'd reach this level of achievement. I particularly love doing brides, angels and glamorous gowns. I hope my dolls inspire others to create, like the artists who inspired me. It is wonderful to create beautiful dolls that touch the hearts of others and I love what I do."

Diamonds and
Roses Angel

Golden Rose

Crystal Roses

DENISE WHITE
Sweetheart Rose Designs
128 N. Gifford, Apt. 2
Elgin, IL 60120

Randy Wilson

Creations by Randy Wilson

"My love affair with vinyl started about ten years ago when I began restoring vintage *BARBIE®* dolls. In those days, there were no books on how to restore and repair dolls so it was mostly trial and error on my part. After numerous experiments, failures and successes, I ended up with a secret stash of horribly disfigured dolls that I prefer to call my mad scientist stage and a new respect for vinyl. Once I finished a group of dolls and was satisfied with their transformation, I sold them on consignment and resumed my search for more victims. As I feared, the day finally arrived when there were no more $12 TNT's to be found and anything vintage was priced at a premium. At that point, I decided to move on and broaden my interests into other types of dolls.

In 1996, a family crisis brought me back to New York where I met a new girl. The local doll shop called 'Angels and Friends' carried the ever-exquisite, elusive *Gene®* doll by designer Mel Odom. Up to this point I had only viewed photos of her in magazines and had not been bitten by the *Gene®* doll bug. When it happened, I fell fast and hard. I sold many of my *BARBIE®* dolls, substituting the *Gene®* doll in their spots. Later that year I also discovered life on the Internet, made many new friends and to my amazement, found that there were many others like me who shared my passion for doll collecting and design. The *Gene®* doll became my next canvas and remains my favorite today. I personally find her much easier to work with simply because of her body size and the quality of her vinyl. I have repainted her, dyed her hair, tinted her body, and even created molded hair for her like the old *Fashion Queen BARBIE®* doll. She still turns out even more beautiful with each new personality.

From the assistance of my sister-in-law who magically transfers my designs from paper to fabric and her undying patience to my partner's talent for designing web pages and my never-ending quest to create the perfect dolls, Wilson Originals has emerged. Most of my creations are currently being sold at an on-line auction on the Internet called eBay.com.

I am truly honored to be included in this book and I hope you enjoy viewing my dolls as much as I enjoyed working on them."

Molded Hair *Gene®* doll

WILSON ORIGINALS
Randy Wilson
306 Princeton Ave.
Corning, N.Y. 14830
E-mail: JRAN2@aol.com
Web Site: http://members.aol.com/jesran/wilson/originals.htm

Cissy as Snow White

Mara Woolf

"Some of my fondest childhood memories are of the many hours my sister and I spent playing with our *BARBIE®* dolls. The high point of our *BARBIE®* doll wardrobe was the many wonderful outfits that were lovingly made by our mom and older sister. I can remember well the Christmas that Santa brought me a children's sewing machine and *BARBIE®* doll patterns! Now I too could sew and make my very own *BARBIE®* doll things. I spent many hours sewing doll outfits and making crocheted hats and stoles. Even when I was "too old" for playing dolls, I continued to make doll clothes for my sister and children's charities for Christmas.

By the time I graduated high school my doll sewing had come to an end since I no longer had anyone's *BARBIE®* dolls to dress. I still had an interest in sewing and design and began to make garments for myself through college and into being a wife and mom. Dolls became a part of my life again after our daughter was born. About the same time that she was ready to begin playing with *BARBIE®* dolls, I discovered the wonderful collector *BARBIE®* dolls that were being made. I soon started a collection and was glad to have the *BARBIE®* doll back in my life. Shortly thereafter, I purchased my first copy of *Barbie Bazaar*

magazine; that issue included an article about the custom dolls of Dick Tahsin. I took one look and said, 'That's what I want to do!' So I started sewing and designing for the *BARBIE®* doll once again. What started out in 1995 as a hobby and a way of personalizing my collection has now blossomed into a full-time venture: 'Mar-a-velous Creations.'

Creations by Mara Woolf

I'd like to think that I inherited my love of sewing and design from my mother and grandmother who were both very talented seamstresses. People always ask me how I do things on such a small scale and where I studied, to which I reply 'It's in my genes.' I haven't had any formal training, just what I learned from Mom.

I feel so lucky that I am able to spend my time doing some-

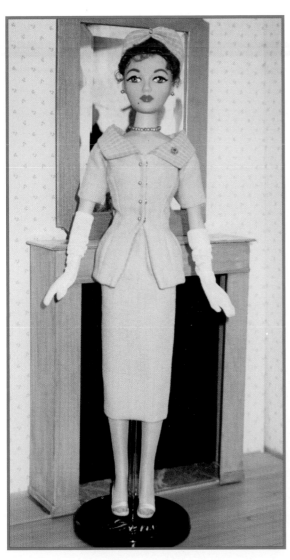

thing that I truly love and enjoy. Every aspect of the process is great, whether it's making the pattern for the outfit, re-rooting and restyling, or changing and repainting the faces. I make sure that each doll and outfit is as perfect as I can possibly make it, and I love to make new accessories to complete the designs.

During the past few months I have been concentrating on designing for the *Gene®* doll - her 'era' and size have added a new dimension to my creativity. I enjoy working with her and will continue to do so. My upcoming *Gene®* doll items will feature some designs that were done by my mom in the 1940s, so they are perfect for the *Gene®* doll. Mom recently passed away, and I plan to reproduce those wonderful designs as a loving tribute to her. My Mom was my greatest 'cheerleader' when it came to my doll projects. I know that she'd be pleased to know that I was selected to be featured in this wonderful book.

Of course, the best part of it all is the nice feeling I get knowing that collectors enjoy the special one-of-a-kind dolls that I create for them. My dolls are bringing smiles to the faces of collectors all over the world! Each doll I make is like a little part of me and sometimes it is hard to part with them. It is great knowing that each will become a unique and loved member of someone's collection. Add to all of this all of the wonderful people that I have met because of my dolls! I can't think of anything I'd rather do! After all, I still have about a million 'Mar-a-velous Creations' in my mind for the future."

MAR-A-VELOUS CREATIONS
Mara Woolf
12400 Rojas #129
El Paso, TX 79927
E-mail: alpha.woolf@worldnet.att.net
Web Site: home.att.net/~alpha.woolf/maravelous/dolls1.htm

Tim Wooten

"My love for *BARBIE®* dolls came at an early age for me, but it wasn't until later in life that I came in contact with the *BARBIE®* doll again and all of the wonderful possibilities she possessed.

I grew up with two sisters who had everything imaginable that Mattel could produce for the *BARBIE®* doll and her friends. I remember the *Malibu BARBIE®* doll being the most special. I, on the other hand, had the *G.I. Joe®* doll, the *Big Jim®* doll and the *Six Million-Dollar Man®* dolls. We usually lived in rural areas so it was up to us to be friends and play with one another. Setting up the *BARBIE®* doll house and playing for hours in a corner of the living room was so much fun for me. I really loved the times we played the day away with the *BARBIE®* doll. Usually, I got stuck making clothes for my sister's dolls or being run out of the *BARBIE®* dollhouse. As we grew up, the *BARBIE®* doll lost her fascination and she was packed away and forgotten...for a time.

When my nieces were born and they became old enough for the *BARBIE®* doll, I couldn't wait to buy them their first dolls. I would run to the local toy store and buy them anything they wanted...still the

Creations by Tim Wooten
Photos by Kelly L. Gamble

Georgia in del Sol

Lindsay in Sweetheart

Alexis High Society

BARBIE® doll bug didn't really bite me until I started seeing the "Holiday Series" at Christmas.

In 1996, I told my mother that I was going to start buying these dolls for collector's sake, but I always waited too long to get one and they were sold out. The next year, she bought me my first one. Then, while on vacation in September 1998, my partner of seven years went to the local K-mart early in the morning and bought me the 1998 *Holiday BARBIE*® doll. This doll really knocked me off my feet and the contagion to own everything the *BARBIE*® doll had hit with a vengeance.

For the next four months, I purchased everything I liked in the *BARBIE*® doll line, and I joined some Internet chat rooms and started one of my own. There, I met a lady named Mary Valderrama. She and I became involved in a swap doll exchange where we would customize a doll for each other around a particular theme. I really had no idea what to do or even where to begin, so I hit the local bookstore for more information. There I found Jim Faraone's two books on *Fashion Doll Makeovers* and saw all the wonderful dolls made by the most creative people I have ever seen.

Mary encouraged me to keep working...I decided at this point to try my hand at customizing a few dolls and putting them on a web site for sale. I finally produced a couple of dolls and a custom box and logo to put on the web site. Now it was time to sit back and wait for the results. Those dolls sold within a couple of days. Shocked, I made more and then more.

Within a couple of weeks, I had a doll nominated as doll of the week on a web site and was chosen first place winner in a Valentine's date contest held at Queen City Collectors Club (in which I also am a member).

My method really isn't that complicated. I start with a trip to the fabric store where ideas seem to jump out at me from the fabric itself. With an idea in mind, I start with the doll's hair. Usually, I remove the head after rolling and doing a boil perm, then set it aside overnight to dry. Then I create the gown or outfit. I do not use patterns so this sometimes is a lengthy process, but I keep at it until it is right. Next, I repaint the eye shadow, lips and even highlight the blush with a shade from the gown. I also always paint the nails and after the paint dries, I seal it with an art glaze to make sure it stays on the doll. While the glaze dries, I begin to make the jewelry, which is my favorite part of the whole process. I like to use natural stones and pieces of glass that I find at a local craft store.

Once the jewelry is made, I put eyelashes on the doll. I use quilter's thread for a full, sensual look. With the bulk of the customization done, I put the doll's head back on and check for total effect. Next, I take the hair down and style it in a fashion that goes with the overall feel of the doll. Next, if needed, I get the shoes ready for the outfit. Sometimes I add beads, but mostly I like to use nail polish with a glitter effect in it to add some life to the plain flat shoe color. Lastly, I create accessories like a wrap, boa or headband; then, construct a handbag or clutch purse to finish the look.

Mary in Hot Rod

All of my dolls come in a custom signed and dated window box and include a stand and usually all accessories as well. My customers seem to really like the presentation of the dolls and the mystery they provide when they first arrive.

Time has passed, but I still love making dolls from my imagination. The joy and comments from my customers creates such a good feeling and I wouldn't trade it for anything. I have been doing some speaking and "how to" classes at doll clubs on the subject of customizing and I have met some wonderful people who really want to learn this art form.

I really could not have done it without the support of my partner Kelly Gamble. I owe a great debt to Mary for her encouraging words, and to Jim for the information to start on what is a great hobby and business."

Dot in Diamond Dazzle

DESIGNS BY TIM
Tim Wooten
4300 Abbeydale Dr.
Charlotte, N.C. 28205
Web Site:
http://hometown.aol.com/tew22/page2/index.htm

Jason Wu

Creations by Jason Wu

"Art, drawing and designing came naturally for me as a toddler. I first discovered the *BARBIE®* doll at the age of three, when she smiled at me at a local department store. Ever since then, I had my mind set on designing for her one day. However, it was not until 1993 with the purchase of my first collectible *BARBIE®* doll, the Bob Mackie *Masquerade Ball®* doll, that I was inspired to design for my favorite fashion doll. Of course, I didn't know how to sew a stitch, so I played around with pieces of fabric, draping it around the doll and then tying it together with ribbons.

A friend and exceptional fashion designer, Tara Zedler, introduced me to sewing in 1994. She has truly inspired and taught me what I have always wanted to pursue. After a period of trial and error, I was finally able to accomplish some simple sheaths and wraps, then eventually I became good at the sewing machine, and that's when my designer dolls came to life. After learning pattern making and sewing, I was inspired by other famous doll artists to do facial repainting and hair styling. Again, after many 'victims,' I successfully achieved the right look with the face and hairstyle.

In 1997, when a new fashion doll, the *Candi®* doll, was introduced, I began designing for her as well. The *Candi®* doll is a truly amazing fashion doll, and no other doll has captured my heart as the *Candi®* doll has. Her multicultural aspects and the wide variety of beautifully sculpted faces kept me wanting for more. I have yet to do a *Gene®* doll, but am working towards using many other fashion dolls as a base for my designer originals. What I look for in my designs are clean lines, luscious fabric and dramatic facial and hair makeover. I tend to enjoy working with fabrics such as silk, satin and chiffon, as the shape and draping of these fabrics often inspires me to do a certain design. When I start a doll, I begin by draping on the doll and creating a pattern. After sewing up a mock, I make the essential modifications, then proceed to the actual dress design. Sometimes a design may take up to five weeks because I want to make sure that everything has the right fit. When I select dolls to work with, I usually choose the *BARBIE*® doll or *Candi*® dolls with the pale, collector skin tones. I enjoy working with the *Candi*® doll faces as well as the 'Mackie' face mold, in addition to the graceful ballerina arms. I am also careful in selecting jewelry for the dolls as well, drawing up different designs first before purchasing the crystals and beads. I design for the pure joy of it, because there is nothing more satisfying than admiring the results after a long, sometimes frustrating process.

The very first exposure of my work was in late 1998, when I sent my dolls to compete in the *Barbie Bazaar*® first annual BMAA competition. I am fortunate and honored to have won first place in both the bridal and the contemporary evening gown categories. Currently, my designs are not for sale, as I treasure each one of my finished products. I consider customizing my free time activity, as I am still concentrating on my studies. I have been blessed to meet many wonderful individuals that have both helped and encouraged me through my artistic interests. My parents have played a large and important role, as they have never given up hope for me. I owe half of my accomplishments to them!"

My BMAA entry, which won first place in the bridal category

JASON WU
4708 Collingwood St.
Vancouver, BC, V6S 2B4
Canada
(860) 687-6697
or
(604) 266-6815
E-mail: poypoy31@yahoo.com

My BMAA entry, which won first place in the contemporary evening gown category.

Escada Shopper (in the collection of Dorothy Fannin)

Vicki Young

Creations by Vicki Young

"One of my earliest memories of my grandmother is of watching her crochet afghans and doilies and make bed doll pillows. At five years old, I began to crochet afghans using the simple crochet stitches that she taught me. A few years later, my mother took me to a nursing home where I visited an elderly lady who taught me to crochet slippers. I spent many cherished hours crocheting and conversing with these two special women.

Also during that time, I, along with my sisters, loved to play with a *BARBIE*® doll. We shared that one doll among the five of us! I would hand/machine sew or crochet simple outfits for that doll.

As I got older, other things took a priority in my life (school, college, marriage, work, etc.) However, I never lost my love for crocheting and dolls. Thus, I began creating crocheted fashion doll heirloom collectibles.

My crocheted collectibles are worn by 11½-inch fashion dolls or smaller. I enjoy creating late 19th and early 20th century costumes and gowns, modern costumes, international costumes, holiday gowns, bridal gowns and baby outfits.

My gowns take anywhere from 15 to 25 hours to complete. They include a crochet pillow form or stand and matching accessories. In addition, I embellish the gowns using feathers, ribbon, pearls and beads.

I always hope that collectors will enjoy owning or giving one of these cherished heirlooms as much as I enjoy crocheting them."

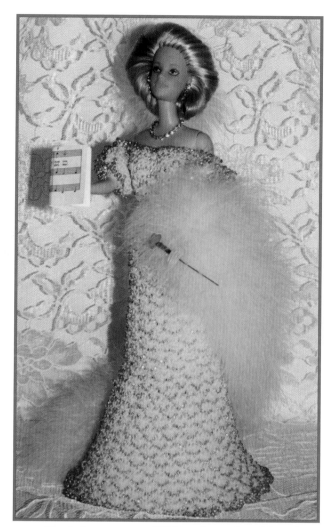

Beaded gown, over 6000 beads crocheted into dress

Molly Brown,
Titanic

Jim Zundel

"My earliest recollection of creating for my fashion doll was as a small child on the floor beside mom watching as she sewed on her machine. I was waiting for whatever scrap she discarded to create a new fashion and fantasy to go with my doll. Creating was the best part of my childhood. I can't recall a time sleeping or awake that I wasn't designing a new ensemble or new persona for my doll. Growing up with beautiful women to inspire me and being surrounded by fashion and accessories meant everything coordinated from head to toe. In my designs I've always felt even the tiniest detail mattered. I am truly blessed with the talent and eye for fashion. In my life I have had enormous support for my work and it continues to inspire me. I am always looking for that thing that will make people notice, whether it is vintage fabrics, accessories or the display stand. I want to convey by my designs that I love what I do. It is a labor of love from start to finish. Design is an adventure; to begin with an idea and bring it to life. I've met a lot of wonderful people who love the fashion doll with as much enthusiasm and have made many new friends. I have sold a lot of my designs and limited editions exclusively at The Doll Collection in Dallas, Texas, where I've found warmth and friendship. Advisedly I would say believe in your dreams, create your fantasies and may they all come true."

Creations by Jim Zundel

J&M TOUCH OF CLASS DESIGNS
Jim Zundel
P.O. Box 1813
Rowlett, TX 75030
E-mail: JandMTOCD@aol.com

HOW TO ENHANCE YOUR OWN FASHION DOLL WONDER

Photos by Kerry Anne Faraone

I have received many letters and E-mails from those interested in knowing how to create different hairstyles on their doll creations. It sounded like a wonderful idea to me, so for you, the artist, I have created this in-depth section on creating different hairstyles.

Before starting any hairstyle featured, make sure you check the doll's rooting from the manufacturer. At times, some rooting features thin hair or bald spots, so you should always comb out a doll's hair to check the rooting and decide if it is suitable for the style you want to achieve.

A little recap from book one: when making a ponytail on a doll, take a strip of hair and wrap it around the rubber band and, using tweezers, pull out a piece of the rubber band and tuck the hair strip under it to hide the rubber band.

When creating tight curls, cut the hair approximately 2 inches from the scalp to make the hair in proportion to the doll. The curlers are actually soda straws cut to the desired length you want. Comb up a strand of hair, cut at an angle and wrap a small rectangular piece of paper toweling to the end to hold the ends in place. Curl the hair on the straw and secure with a pearl-tipped pin.

Remember to boil the hair in a pot of boiling water for only 15 seconds.

Tools needed: Comb, paper towel, scissors, needle and thread, clear contact paper, straight pins, styling gel, straws, coffee stirrers, pipe cleaners, wire, pearl tipped pins, fabric tack glue, sponge hair curlers, acrylic paint, paint brush, water, bowl, bobby pins, beads, masking tape, duct tape, acrylic modeling paste and tweezers.

Spiral or Banana Curls

Step 1

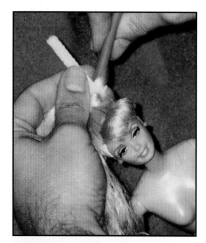

Step 2

Step 3

Step 4

Start by wetting the doll's hair and making a ponytail either in the back or on the top of the doll's head. Take a long soda straw and measure the desired length by taking a strip of hair and wrapping it down the straw and snipping off the excess length of the straw. **(Step 1)** Take a pipe cleaner and insert it into the straw with both ends of the pipe cleaner extending beyond the ends of the straw. **(Step 2)** Wrap the end of the pipe cleaner close to the scalp to hold it in place. This will make your spiral curls start right at the hairline. **(Step 3)** Take a strip of wet hair (if desired, you can comb in a tiny bit of styling gel), and keeping the hair flat, wrap it down along the soda straw. **(Step 4)** When the hair reaches the bottom of the soda straw, bend up the pipe cleaner extending out of the bottom of the straw and wrap it around the hair at the bottom to hold it in place. **(Step 5)** Continue this with all the hair strips, then place the pearl-tipped pins into the top of the straws and into the scalp to hold them in place. Boil the hair in bubbling hot water for just 15 seconds, blot it dry with a towel and allow to dry overnight. (When boiling hairstyles using pipe cleaners, always support the doll's head when it comes out of the water. The weight of the wet pipe cleaners can damage the neck knob and no one likes a wobbly doll head) **(Step 6)** Once

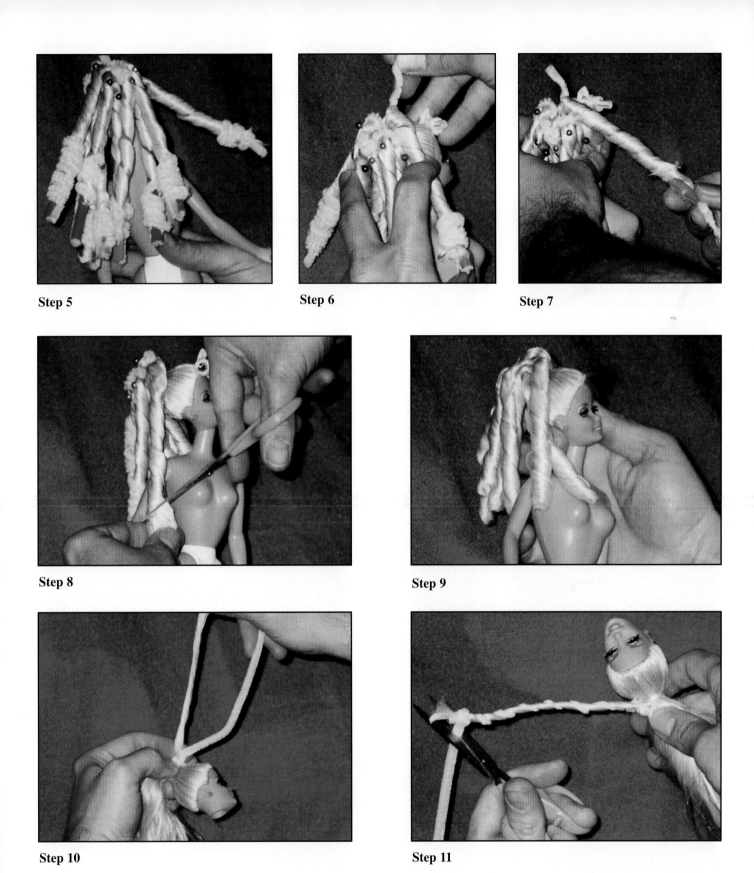

Step 5

Step 6

Step 7

Step 8

Step 9

Step 10

Step 11

the hair is thoroughly dry, remove the pearl-tipped pin at the top and carefully unwind the pipe cleaner at the scalp. **(Step 7)** Untwist the pipe cleaner at the bottom of the straw and very carefully remove the pipe cleaner by pulling it through the straw from the bottom. Carefully untwist the hair from the straw. **(Step 8)** Snip off the sometimes frizzy end of the hair. **(Step 9)** Continue this with all the curls until you have a beautiful set of curls cascading down your doll's back.

Extra tips: **(Step 10)** If you desire teeny, tight cascading curls, just forget the straw and fasten a pipe cleaner to the scalp and wrap the hair along the pipe cleaner. **(Step 11)** Fasten it at the bottom and cut the excess pipe cleaner. Boil it, let it dry and remove the pipe cleaners.

Grecian Curls

Step 12

Step 13

Step 14

Step 15

Step 16

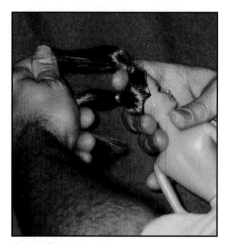

Step 17

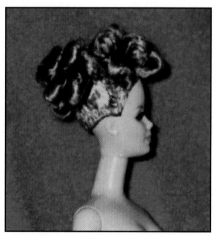

Step 18

(**Step 12**) Start with a ponytail at the top of the head. Wet the hair and use the cut soda straws, paper towels and pins to roll a circle of hair around the base of the ponytail. (Remember to cut the hair at an angle or cut it in an arrow shape 2 inches from the scalp.) Roll the hair down toward the hairline and secure with a pearl-tipped pin. (**Step 13**) Now set another circle of hair above the first circle, rolling the hair once again down toward the hairline. (**Step 14**) Finish setting the last of the ponytail on top of the doll's head and snip any loose or flyaway hairs that you can see. (Snipping these loose hairs is important as you work on your doll's hair and should be done every so often.) Boil the doll's hair for 15 seconds, blot dry and let it dry thoroughly overnight. (**Step 15**) Once the hair is dry, carefully remove the pin and slowly unwind the straw from the head. (**Step 16**) Now you have your doll looking like an ode to a Grecian doll.

Extra tips: You can place the ponytail on your doll at the nape of the neck for a sophisticated look or at the top of the forehead for a Betty Grable look and set the hair the same way as mentioned previously. (**Step 17**) Also try making 2 or 3 ponytails along the doll's scalp and setting each ponytail as previously described and you will have a row of Grecian curls along the doll's head. (**Step 18**).

Artichoke and Bubble Cut

Step 19

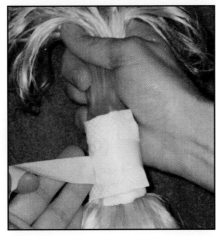

Step 20

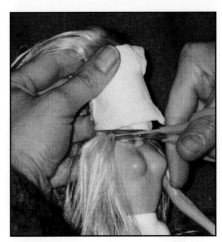

Step 21

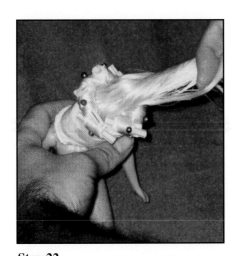

Step 22

Step 23

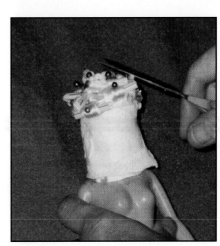

Step 24

(**Step 19**) Wet the hair and comb down one row of the hair at the hairline all around the doll's head. (**Step 20**) Fold a paper towel into a strip and wrap it around the doll's head to secure the combed down hair. Wrap masking tape around the paper towel several times to hold it in place. (**Step 21**) Cut the hair sticking out of the bottom of the paper towel. (**Step 22**) Now roll the hair on top of the head in a circle down toward the hairline. (**Step 23**) Once again, do another circle of rolled curls toward the hairline and (**Step 24**) finish curling the top and snip off the loose and fly- away hairs. Place the doll's head in the pot of boiling water for just 15 seconds, blot dry, and allow the hair and paper towel to dry thoroughly. (**Step 25**)

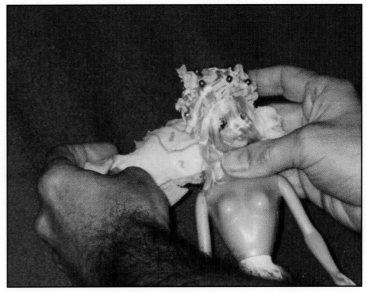

Step 25

Step 26

Step 27

Step 28

Step 29

Step 30

Once everything is dry, remove the tape and paper towel from the doll's face and **(Step 26)** slowly and carefully cut the doll's bangs at the eyebrows, continuing around below the ears and along the nape of the neck. **(Step 27)** Carefully unset the hair and, using your fingers, feather out each curl or **(Step 28)** with a comb, take each curl separately and slowly run your comb through it once or twice, but no more than that. More combing would result in a frizz and you wouldn't want that. **(Step 29)** Again, clip any flyaway hairs, or clip a little at a time to shape the doll's hairstyle to your liking. For the Bubble Cut, just eliminate Steps 19, (except for wetting the hair) 20 and 21. Roll the hair in circles right at the hairline and finish the top. **(Step 30)** You will then have your Bubble Cut ready for a day at the beach.

Straight Hair and Pixie Cut

(Step 31) Wet the hair and comb it straight down. **(Step 32)** If you want bangs to the side, comb the front of the hair to the side and hold it in place. **(Step 33)**

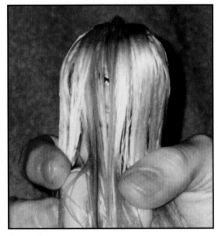

Step 31

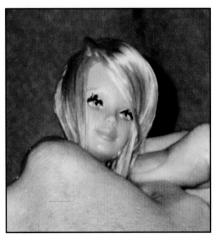

Step 32

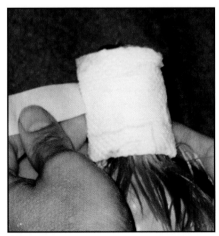

Step 33

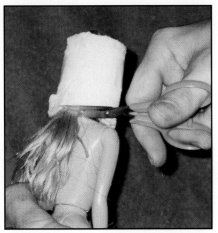

Step 34

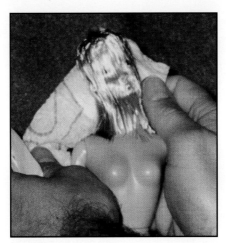

Step 35

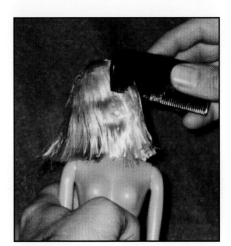

Step 36

Step 37

Wrap the folded paper towel around the doll's head and fasten with masking tape to hold the hair in place. **(Step 34)** Cut the hair sticking out of the bottom of the paper towel and boil the doll's head for the 15 seconds and blot dry. **(Step 35)** Once the hair and paper towel are dry, remove the tape and paper towel **(Step 36)** and comb the hair down. **(Step 37)** Now slowly and carefully, cut the doll's bangs at her eyebrows. For a longer look cut the doll's hair at the shoulder. For the Pixie Cut **(Step 38)**, keep the bangs at the eyebrows or a little shorter and cut the hair along the bottom of the ear and at the nape of the neck. Do this very slowly and cut only a fraction at a time. If the hair seems thick in the back, just lift the top layer of hair and cut the under layers a bit shorter so it will lay straight. To shape it even more, cut just the top layer a fraction shorter than the layer below to give it a rounded look. This is probably one of the most difficult hairstyles to do, but if you take your time, I have faith that you can achieve it **(Step 39)** and have your own Peter Pan look-a-like.

Step 38

Step 39

Twisted Curls

Step 40

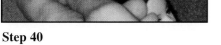

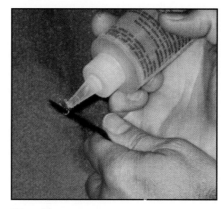

Step 41

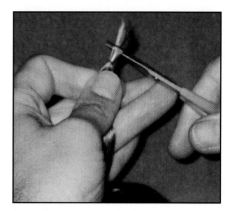

Step 42

Step 43

Step 44

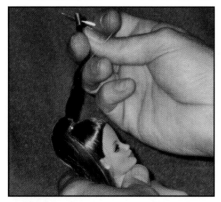

Step 45

Step 46

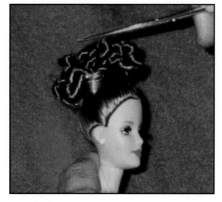

Step 47

Wet the hair and put it into a ponytail. **(Step 40)** Take a strip of hair and comb it up and tie the end of it with thread. **(Step 41)** Take some fabric tack glue and go around the knotted thread to hold it in place and to hold the hairs together. Continue now with more strips of hair. **(Step 42)** Once the glue has thoroughly dried, take a thin strip of clear contact paper and wrap it around the glued thread. (I used silver duct tape here so you can see what is being done.) Then snip the end of the hair through the clear contact paper and continue with the other strips of hair. **(Step 43)** Insert a pin halfway through the clear contact paper **(Step 44)** and by holding the pin, pull the hair and twist it in a clockwise movement until the hair feels too tight to twist anymore. **(Step 45)** Without letting go, take the pin and insert it close to the ponytail and into the scalp. You will see that the twisted hair curls up nicely to give a wonderful effect. **(Step 46)** Continue with the next strip, pinning it close to the previous one. **(Step 47)** Take your last remaining strip of hair and wrap it around the exposed clear contact paper ends to hide them and pin it under the hair. Remember to clip any flyaway hairs that you see.

Braids, Braids, Braids

Step 48

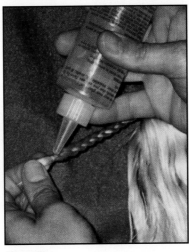

Step 49

Step 50

Step 51

Step 52

(**Step 48**) Wet the doll's hair (you can also use styling gel) and judge how many braids you want to make on the doll's head. Divide up those sections and starting with the first section, begin to braid the hair. (**Step 49**) Once you have completed braiding the first braid, tie it off with a piece of thread and run the fabric tack glue around it like with the Twisted Curls. (**Step 50**) Once the glue has dried, wrap the clear contact paper around it and snip off the end. This is also a good time to clip any flyaway hairs from the braid. (**Step 51**) Once all the braids are done, take each finished braid and insert a straight pin into the clear contact paper, around the base of the braid and into the scalp. (**Step 52**) Wrap the last braid around the base of the braids to hide the clear contact paper and pins. Secure the end under the wrapped braid and pin into place. (**Step 53**) Once again, snip any fly- away hairs and she's ready for a night on the town.

Step 53

Step 54

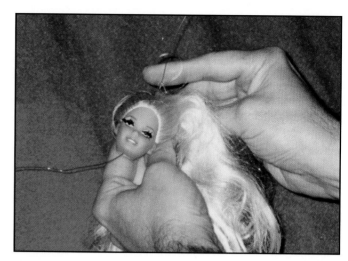

Step 55

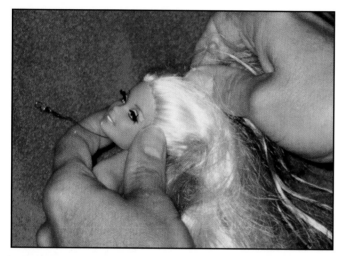

Step 56

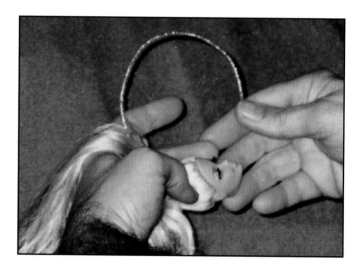

Step 57

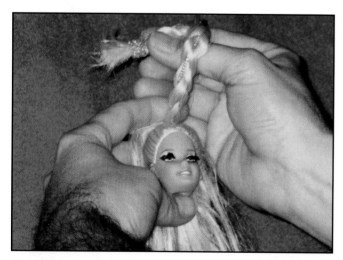

Step 58

Extra tips: (**Step 54**) If you find your final braid will not wrap around the base of the braids, you can use some seam binding (or decorative trim) to hide the pins and clear contact paper. (**Step 55**) To make wire braids, first remove the doll's head. At the point where you're going to start the ponytail for the braids, insert a wire from outside the head, through the head and out the neck opening. (**Step 56**) Attach a small seed bead to the end of the wire and pull the wire back up from the top of the head. This will secure the wire in place. Decide how many braids you want to do and put in that number of wires (one for each braid). Make your ponytail and then braid each piece of hair around the wire and finish it up as described for the braids previously. (**Step 57**) If you want to get fancy, string some beads onto those wires. Braid the beaded wire into the hair and wrap the end of the beaded wire to hold it into place. (**Step 58**) Also with braids, if you braid the hair and boil it for the 15 seconds, blot dry, let it dry and then take out the braids, you will have a fun and easy rippled effect to the doll's hair.

Flip and Page Boy

(**Step 59**) For the Flip, wet the dolls' hair and comb it down. Wrap the folded paper towel (secured with masking tape) onto her forehead as if the doll has a headache (who wouldn't after having their hair pulled and yanked all different ways). You may want to add two pearl-tipped pins through the paper towel and into her scalp (never the doll's face) to hold the taped paper towel in place during the boiling. (**Step 60**) Comb a section of hair, wrap the end with a small piece of paper towel and roll upward on the straw. (**Step 61**) You never want to put a pin into a doll's face because it will definitely leave a mark. To hold this straw curler in place, insert a piece of pipe cleaner through the straw and (**Step 62**) fold the two ends of the pipe cleaner toward each other to secure the curler in place. (This pipe cleaner method to hold the doll's curlers in place works very well on the harder vinyl dolls such as the *Gene*® doll where a pin is nearly impossible to get into her scalp. It is also great for children who want to redesign their dolls without the dangers of getting stuck with the pins.) (**Step 63**) Continue this for about 5 sections of hair and when done, boil the hair for the 15 seconds and blot dry. (**Step 64**) When completely dried, remove the taped paper towel and carefully undo the pipe cleaner and curler from each section. (**Step 65**) Insert your finger into the curl and slowly and carefully comb each section just once or twice to bring the sections all together. (**Step 66**) And there you have a flip that would make "That Girl" giggle with delight.

For the PageBoy, follow the same directions and just roll the hair under and secure with pipe cleaners. It's as easy as that!

Step 59

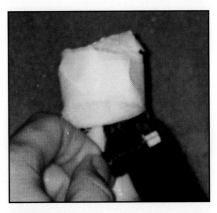

Step 60

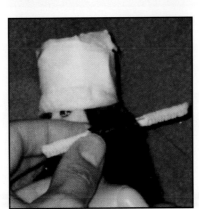

Step 61

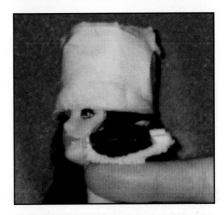

Step 62

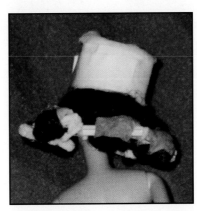

Step 63

Step 64

Step 65

Step 66

Soft Page Boy

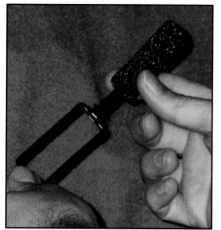

Step 67

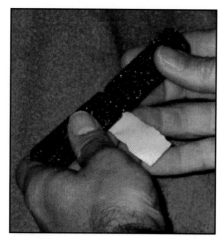

Step 68

Step 69

Step 70

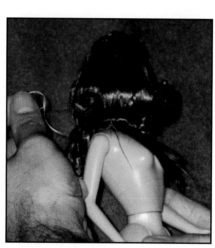

Step 71

(**Step 67**) Remove the sponge from two sponge hair curlers and (**Step 68**) secure them together well with duct tape. (Wrap the tape around the sponges a few times so they don't loosen up when boiling the hair.) (**Step 69**) Lift the doll's hair and wrap the sponge around the doll's lower face and secure the ends together with a pearl-tipped pin. (**Step 70**) Comb the doll's hair down over the sponges and, using thread, tie the hair around the doll's neck. Boil the hair for 15 seconds (This time when the water boils, turn off the heat and let the water stop bubbling before dipping the head into the water. This way the action of the bubbles won't mess up the hair too much.), blot it and let it dry thoroughly. This may take a little longer to dry since the sponge will hold some water. (**Step 71**) Once the hair and sponge are dry, cut the thread securing the hair to the doll's neck. You will see that the hair has a permanent crease where the thread was and this is your cutting line. (**Step 72**) Cut along that creased line and before you know it, you have (**Step 73**) a soft, pageboy for that spring afternoon.

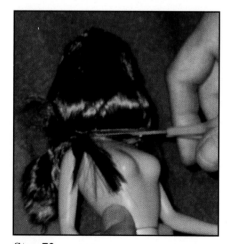

Step 72

Step 73

Braids and Curls

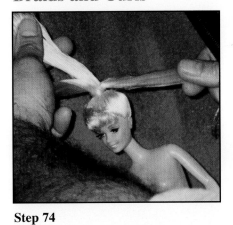

Step 74

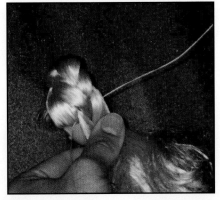

Step 75

Step 76

It's also fun to combine styles also. **(Step 74)** Start with a ponytail at the top of the head, wet the hair and braid it until it reaches the nape of the neck. **(Step 75)** Where the braid reaches the nape of the neck, tie it together with some thread to hold it. **(Step 76)** Then take a needle and thread and where the braid ends, insert the needle through the back of the hair on the doll, along the width of the braid, and tie the braid down to the doll's head. **(Step 77)** The remaining hair from the end can then be set like you set the hair for the Grecian Curls and secured with the pearl-tipped pins. Boil the hair for 15 seconds, blot dry and let it dry overnight. **(Step 78)** Remove the curlers and you have a fun and inventive hairstyle combining two techniques.

Step 77

Step 78

Split Curls

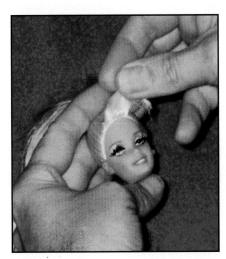

Step 79

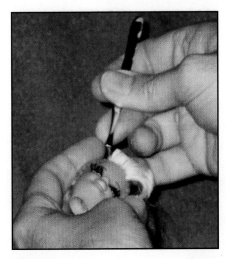

Step 80

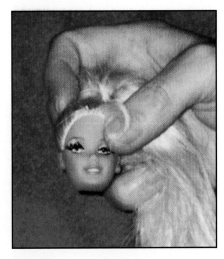

Step 81

(Step 79) Before you attempt this, make sure that the bangs on you doll are rooted behind the hairline. Otherwise you'll have a few bald spots where you don't want them. Once you establish that the bangs are rooted behind the hairline, **(Step 80)** you can pluck the hairs out that you don't want with a pair of tweezers and get that single spit curl swooping over the doll's forehead. **(Step 81)**

Dying The Hair

Step 82

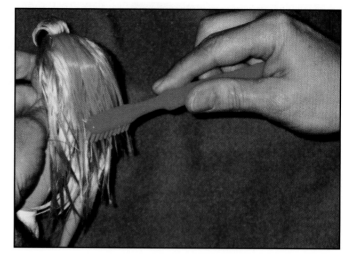
Step 83

Step 84

Step 85

Step 86

Dying the hair can be quite tricky because you never know what the future may bring. Whatever I publish in my "How To" sections, I have waited at least 10 years to see what effect the process has on the dolls. I have heard that a few are dying their dolls' hair with marking pens, dyes, and some pretty scary other things and though it may work great now, it may cause some problems down the road. At one time, I signed the back of my dolls' heads with permanent markers. They worked great for a long time, but after about 6 years, I noticed that the permanent marker slowly bled its way into the vinyl.

The only dyeing I believe in (although you can reroot your dolls with wild colored hair found at beauty supply shops) is using acrylic paint. I did this 10 years ago, and the first doll I entered in a competition had pink hair, which got a few chuckles from the judges, plus a ribbon. Since we paint the dolls' faces with acrylic paint, we know that over time it does not bleed into the vinyl.

Always use a shiny-haired doll for this process, which works out much better. **(Step 82)** Put some acrylic paint into a bowl of water and stir it well until the paint is completely dissolved. You will need a light blonde doll for this and **(Step 83)**, using a hard or medium toothbrush, dip the toothbrush into the bowl of watered-down acrylic paint and comb it through the doll's hair. Keep a paper towel with you and anytime some of the paint gets onto the doll's hairline or skin, wipe it off immediately. Since the paint is thinned down, it will wipe off easily, but do it right away and don't allow it to dry. **(Step 84)** Spread the hair as you go to make sure that all the hair is coated. I usually like to use a small amount of paint in the hair because I like the contrast of light and dark shades, but that is up to you. **(Step 85)** Once you're finished getting the color you desire, (mainly this technique will give you pastel colors) set the doll upside down and comb the hair every few minutes while it is drying. This will keep the hair from getting too stiff and if you watered down the paint thin enough, you should be able to have some fun creating a total new look for your dolls. **(Step 86)**

Molded Hair

A special thanks to featured fashion doll makeover artist Dorothy Fannin for sharing her instructions and tips for doing molded hair dolls.

Step 87

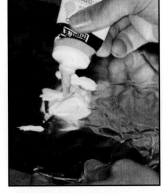

Step 88

Step 89

Step 90

As done for rerooting, remove the doll's head, cut the doll's hair as short as you can and pluck out the hairs inside the head with tweezers as described in the first book. Once the doll's head is completely and thoroughly clean of any hair **(Step 87)**, put some of the acrylic modeling paste onto your finger (you can also use a thin paint brush if you have stubby fingers) and cover the doll's head with it to cover the holes where the hair was rooted. Let this dry thoroughly. **(Step 88)** Put some of the acrylic modeling paste on some foil and mix in the color acrylic paint that you want. **(Step 89)** Using a wide-tipped brush **(Step 90)**, start painting the doll's hair, being careful not to get it onto the forehead or ears. (Always have a toothpick on hand to scoop away the mixture where you don't want it.) Let this dry and then the fun begins. **(Step 91)** Using a thicker amount of the mixture, begin designing your hairstyle by applying a thicker amount of modeling paste and building it up as you go. You can let your imagination run wild with this fun technique and achieve a unique **(Step 92)** looking creation that work well with everything from grunge-type outfits to haute couture. You can let this dry and then build more on your hairstyle if desired. Also, if you don't achieve the exact color you wanted, you can repaint the doll's molded hair when completely dried.

Extra tips: You can use the metallic or pearlized acrylic paints that are used for T-shirts to give your molded hairstyle a nice, shiny look. Or look for an acrylic glaze to coat the matte finish to the hair, although the matte hair looks just as good on a doll. I have been experimenting with this myself, and using thin strips of buckram, I have been making curls (loops) and sewing them in place onto the doll's head. Then I coat them with the modeling paste. Once dried, I build the hairstyle up with the paint mixture. I have also sewn various sized beads onto the doll's head and then coated them with the modeling paste **(Step 93)**. This is a technique that can really get your creative juices flowing.

Once you have all these techniques done **(Step 94)**, the fun begins with designing for those fashion doll wonders.

Step 91

Step 92

Step 93

Now you have several ideas on how to create the look you want on your dolls. The fun part is experimenting and the sharing of ideas. No one alone can learn everything, but as a group we can all learn together. Stay positive with things and keep positive people around you. Find a group that works well together with sharing ideas and not one that is more into competing with or criticizing other artists. Negativeness can drain your creative energies and that's the last thing you want to do. Save your energy for creating wonderful creations and improving your techniques. Please be careful of some of the tips you may get on how to makeover your dolls. I have heard a few tips on the Internet that will ruin your dolls down the line. Make sure the individual giving the advice knows what he or she is doing and has tested the techniques for the long run. If you hear of a technique and are not sure about it, always feel free to contact me and I'll let you know what I know about the technique.

Fashion doll makeovers have come a long way from when they first started many years ago. Although many magazines have featured the artists over the years, since my books have come out, you see that more and more of the magazines are now featuring "How To" sections, which I think is wonderful! The point is to share ideas and to help each other along the bumpy road. But, most of all, have fun with what you are doing and you will turn that bumpy road into a smooth riding creative experience.

Jim Faraone
19109 Silcott Springs Rd.
Purcellville, VA 20132
(540) 338-3621
E-mail: jimfaraone@erols.com
Web Site: http://www.erols.com/jimfaraone/

Do You Have These Books?

Fashion Doll Makeovers

Delve into the fascinating world of Fashion Doll Makeovers with 34 of the hottest artists' creations. Instructional for rerooting hair, painting faces, remodeling hands, arms, feet, designing an outfit, accessorizing, and marketing. A full color Makeover Extravaganza! 281 Color photos. **112 pages. 8-1/2" x 11". PB. Item #H5245. (0-87588-471-7). $19.95**

2nd Fashion Doll Makeovers

One of the hottest trends in the doll world today is the making over of popular dolls. This volume demonstrates how a creative touch can transform an average-looking doll into a glamorous showgirl, a fashion statement, or even a whimsical creature of fantasy. 50 artists from all over the world have sent examples of their latest work. A chapter "How to Create Your Own Fashion Wonder" explains how to make recreations. 200+ color photos. **112 pages. 8-1/2" x 11". PB. Item #H5458. (0-87588-515-2). $19.95**

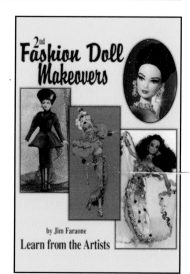